SEEKIN
OUR
EAGLE

by

Karen Charlton

The genealogical research behind
Catching the Eagle

SEEKING OUR EAGLE

ISBN 978-0-9928-0369-8

karencharlton1@gmail.com

Alternatively, the author can be contacted through her website:

www.karencharlton.com

Visit Karen Charlton's website to learn more about her historical novels. While there, sign up for Karen Charlton's FREE monthly newsletter and join in discussion on her blog.

www.karencharlton.com

For Beth and Ross

My much-loved
pair of little 'villains'.

Here's a unique history of your own.

And for my darling, Chris.
Thank you for the journey, my love.
xxx

ACKNOWLEDGEMENTS

My first set of grateful thanks must go to our Charlton cousins, who all gave permission to use photographs and narrative from the family archives in the production of this book. Thanks to Jackie Charlton, daughter of Raymond, for many of the photographs and to Patricia Batterley (neé Charlton) daughter of James Mervyn Charlton, to use the extracts and photographs from her father's books *Sand in my Shoes* and *More Sand in my Shoes*. I would also like to thank Annie's sons (who don't want to be named) for permission to use the lovely photograph of their Mum, and Iain Wolstencroft who took many of the modern photographs which illustrate this book.

My quirky book cover has been designed by the extremely patient David Harland at Q Design, Middlesbrough. Thank you for your friendship and tolerance, David.

I also need to thank Babs, June, Kristin, Jean, Sam Blain (*His Excellency the Cultural Attaché for Boosbeck*) and Moon for valuable feedback regarding the content and style of this book. Thank you also to Jill Boulton for both her unwavering friendship over the past twenty-five years and for editing the manuscript and to Sandra Mangan for the proofread. Thank you all.

Last but not least, I would like to thank my long-suffering family, Chris, Beth and Ross, for their patience and resilience during the months it took to write yet *another* book.

We may not have a 'family pile', kids, but one of these days this writing malarkey will make us rich. Failing that, if you're up for a spot of burglary, I've still got the postcode for Kirkley Hall on the sat nav.

Praise for *Seeking Our Eagle*

Love of family is what drives all research into our ancestry, and love of her family shines through every fascinating detail of Karen Charlton's detective work into the English Border clan of the Charltons. She wasn't expecting to shake the family tree and have a 19th century convict fall out of it but she tracked Bad Granddad (the Great, four times removed) through dusty records and even dustier Northumberland lanes, pursuing the truth like a bloodhound employed by her fictional Detective Lavender. There is something in this warm, funny, practical book for everyone.

Jean Gill, author of *Song at Dawn*

This fascinating story of a family's search for their ancestors certainly proves that truth is stranger than fiction. A great complement to *Catching the Eagle.*

Kristin Gleeson, author of *Selkie Dreams*
and *Anahareo: A Wilderness Spirit*

Having read Karen Charlton's debut novel, *Catching the Eagle*, I eagerly awaited the book that would explain the remarkable string of events which led the Charlton family to discover a skeleton in the closet and a notable miscarriage of justice. I was not disappointed.

This is not merely an account of genealogical research. It is a warm invitation from a very real and vibrant author, to accompany her and her family as they embark on a remarkable journey of discovery. Assisted by lively and often humorous narration and poignant photographs, we are given a glimpse of the harsh and trying lives endured by our Northern ancestors. We peep into scenes of great national pride, with the building of the railways, and heartache at the loss of cherished children. Poverty, sadness, joy and adversity are keenly illustrated as social history unfolds through the lives of the Charlton clan.

Whether you come upon this book before, or after, reading *Catching the Eagle*, this is without doubt a wonderful accompaniment. A must for all those with a need to know why we are who we are, and how we are shaped by the events experienced by those who lived before us.

B. A. Morton, author of *Mrs Jones* and *Wildewood*

CONTENTS

FOREWORD

In 2004, my husband and I made a fantastic discovery.

While researching his family history, we found a jailbird roosting in the branches of our ancestral tree.

We discovered that Jamie Charlton, my husband's four times great-grandfather, had been tried and convicted of an audacious burglary in Northumberland back in 1810. Originally sentenced to death, Jamie's punishment had later been commuted to transportation to New South Wales in Australia.

If the truth be told, most of us hope to discover a bit of mystery when we undertake genealogical research. The odd skeleton in the cupboard or some salacious gossip we can share with friends over a drink in the pub. Illegitimacy, desertion or even a bigamist will not go amiss. It all adds to the excitement of the search. *Who Do You Think You Are?* a phenomenally successful TV series, is based on our curiosity about ancestors.

But I don't think anything can prepare anyone for the surprise when a convict drops out of the family tree. Yes, our Australian cousins probably brace themselves to discover a felon or two in their heritage, but this does not happen on a regular basis for the average Brit. We tend to forget that many of those men and women transported to Australia left their families behind in Britain and Ireland.

However, Jamie Charlton was not just any old criminal. We researched his case for years, hunting down every scrap of information available about the burglary at Kirkley Hall and we quickly realised that his conviction was a dodgy one – even by the questionable legal standards of 1810. We had our very own Regency miscarriage of justice.

I had always wanted to write books and I soon started to appreciate that the perfect plot for a historical novel had just landed in my lap. In fact, we had gathered enough information for a whole series of books about this devastating trauma faced by Jamie and his family. Our research had uncovered a tale worth telling and I knew that if I didn't settle down to write this story, I would never achieve my lifetime ambition of becoming a novelist.

Catching the Eagle took twenty-six months to write and was eventually published by Knox Robinson, publishers of historical fiction, in December 2011.

After the book launch, the interest in the background to the novel took me by surprise. Newspapers, radio and even a TV station all wanted to know how we had discovered our unusual skeleton in the closet. Genealogy groups, libraries and local historical societies invited me to talk about the subject, an experience I thoroughly enjoyed. I soon realised there might also be a wider audience for this extraordinary story and decided to write a complementary factual book, called *Seeking Our Eagle*, which mapped our genealogical experience and my creative journey into fiction.

This is it. This is the story of how an interest in genealogy changed our lives.

This is the story of how we searched for our eagle.

The book launch of 'Catching the Eagle'.

CHAPTER ONE
Charlton Robbers and Raiders – pre-17th century

In the heart of a Northumbrian town called Hexham, on an elevated spot above the black and meandering River Tyne, stands a huge, rectangular building known as Hexham Old Gaol. Now a museum, it was the first purpose-built prison in England.

Hexham Old Gaol

At dusk, it looms out of the twilight like an impenetrable fortress as you trudge up the steep hill from the car park below. The ground floor is a near-windowless solid wall of rough-hewn, ancient stone laid several feet thick. Erected in the early 14th century, Hexham Old Gaol was used as a prison for almost 500 years.

Not many people voluntarily go to prison during their leisure time but in the summer of 1995, we did. My husband, Chris, announced that he wanted to call in and visit this gloomy stronghold on our way up to Kielder in Northumberland. We had set off for a short walking holiday and the car was weighed down with hiking boots, wet-weather gear, a travel cot and the rest of the paraphernalia which goes with a travelling infant and a week's holiday in the British Isles.

I checked on our sleeping daughter in the back of the car, then stretched out my legs, kicked off my sandals beneath the dashboard and admired the incredible beauty of the rural landscape around us. The sun shone and a vast expanse of ice-blue, northern sky arched above us.

'Why?' I asked. 'Why go to this old prison?'

'It has a good museum about the Border Reivers.'

'Remind me again: who are they?'

Chris turned down the volume on the car CD. Bruce Springsteen faded into the background.

'The reivers were roving gangs – families – of villains and thieves who terrorised the Border region between Scotland and England before the two countries united under James I.'

'Nice. Medieval anarchists.'

He ignored my sarcasm.

'Every now and then, these families would gather in large numbers, mount their horses and thunder across the border to raid the farms of the Scots.'

'How did the Scots feel about this?'

Dark sunglasses hid his eyes. I watched him in profile as his strong jawline relaxed and a wide grin spread across his handsome face.

'They got their own back.'

'I bet they did.'

'It was a tough time in history. They were a hard people who lived in harsh times – lawless and violent.'

I glanced at him again, my curiosity piqued. Was he trying to justify this thievery?

'The two opposing armies of Scotland and England frequently burnt this area to the ground. It reminds me a bit of the American Wild West frontier.'

I smiled. My gentle-giant of a husband clearly romanticised this gang of thugs.

'The Charltons of the North Tyne Valley were one of the largest of these families of thieves and cattle rustlers.'

'Humph!' I teased. 'My grandmother always said you were a 'wrong 'un'.'

This was true. Gladys had been eighty-five when she first met Chris. She suffered from dementia and lived in a nursing home. She took one glance at my future husband, declared that he was a 'wrong 'un' and promptly fell back to sleep. I went ahead and married him anyway but it's not the kind of thing a girl forgets.

'Anyway, I think this is where my ancestors came from. I'd like to try and find out more about the Charltons from Hexham museum.'

'But your Dad said your ancestors came from County Durham. They all worked as railway stationmasters, didn't they?'

'Last century, yes,' Chris explained, patiently. 'Most Charltons originate from Northumberland. The Charlton reivers lived *five hundred* years ago.'

I nodded and settled back in my seat. I felt myself relax as the distance increased between us and our humdrum existence of work and child-rearing back in Teesside. Northumberland had always been one of our favourite places in the world. We loved its beauty, its castles and its empty, winding country lanes. The next few days stretched endlessly before us, an exciting blank canvas which we could fill with whatever adventures and experiences we chose. Northumberland smiled and beckoned us towards its turbulent medieval history.

Chris's interest in the Charlton family history had begun when our daughter, Beth, was born and now I was beginning to share his curiosity. I believe there's something about having children which not only makes you look forward to the future, but also makes you wonder about where your little one came from. We knew this tiny stranger in our arms was the latest in a long line of Charltons, but who were those shadowy figures in history that had passed down her surname and contributed to her genetic makeup? What were their stories? We wanted to give our children a history which was uniquely theirs.

Of course, to a child, Mum's family is as important as Dad's, but my father had already begun the frustrating job of researching my own family tree. His difficult experiences had made me wary of this genealogy malarkey. My own ancestry heaved with dubious marriages, several generations of illegitimacy and unexplained name changes. The records showed that our family had roamed south from Norfolk to London then, after a hasty name change, headed sharply north to Lancashire and Yorkshire. My Dad eventually concluded that they were either on the run from the constables or involved in a witness protection scheme. It also appeared that half of them had been abducted by aliens.

In terms of an interesting and unique history, my own ancestry had too many problems and gaps to be considered an enjoyable or suitable story for our children. But no-one at that point had investigated the Charlton line, and despite being an anathema to ardent feminists, the lure and mystery of the traditional, paternal surname is very, very strong.

When Chris and I finally reached Hexham Old Gaol and museum, we found it fascinating. It gave us a wonderful insight into prison life in medieval times and the era of the Border Reivers. The interactive exhibits brought them alive.

The Charltons were featured in the museum. They, along with the Milburns, the Robsons and the others, came across as an independent breed of people who didn't care about anyone or anything not connected to their own tribes. I read about one harassed border official who declared: 'They are people that will be Scottish when they will and English at their pleasure.'

We learnt that the reivers moved only at night. They took advantage of their intimate knowledge of the remote and rugged terrain to spirit away their ill-gotten plunder. The two warring governments of Scotland and England were complicit in this state of attrition; it suited them to have gangs of outlaws harassing the enemy on the border. But nobody – not even royalty – dared to travel through this lawless area without armed protection. Apart from robbery, kidnap and blackmail – murder was also common.

I later discovered that the name 'Charlton' means 'free peasant' or 'peasant of the free town'. A 'free peasant' was a rarity in a medieval England ground down by feudalism. It implies that our surname sprang from a person, or group of people, who refused to accept the rule of their Norman masters. It has also been suggested that the word 'Charl' is a corruption of 'churl' from churlish. When I combine these two definitions, it evokes a wonderful image of a load of bad-tempered, rebellious yokels, fed up with the constant decimation of their farmland by first one side and then the other, in the continuous war between the Scots and their English overlords. It's no wonder this area and history created 'free peasants' and Border Reivers.

The peasants revolted, became a law unto themselves and the Borderlands became an uncontrollable 'no-man's land'.

We scrambled up the stairs to the small room near the top of the gaol. Several ancient tomes lay scattered across a battered, wooden table beneath a glass case. Badly-typed transcripts rubbed shoulders with illegible, original documents. We peered down at close-writ, spidery handwriting and faded ink.

'Look at this!' Chris exclaimed. 'This fellah reckons there were at least six hundred Charlton men 'without hoss' who lived in the North Tyne valley in the fourteenth century.'

I padded across to stand next to him and peer in the direction of his pointed finger.

'What's a hoss?'

'Horse.'

'So, if there were six hundred Charltons 'without hoss'; how many of them had a hoss?'

'It doesn't say.'

My brain began to calculate.

'If we take into account the women and children – and the men with hosses – there must have been over a thousand Charltons alive in this valley back then.'

I paused for a moment and went to sit down on the uneven window-seat in the thick walls. Behind me the sunlight streamed in through the grimy panes.

'That's one hell of a lot of Charltons for just one valley,' I added, thoughtfully.

'Yes, and some of them will have been related to us.' His voice now assumed the smug, velvet tone it always acquired when Middlesbrough F.C. win a football match.

Beth woke up and demanded food. While I gave a bottle of lukewarm milk to the future of the Charltons, Chris continued to wallow in their past. He worked his way round the rest of the old manuscripts.

'Here's a good story,' he informed me over his shoulder. 'There was a gadgie called Topping Charlton – a notorious law-breaker. They caught him and imprisoned him, here – in Hexham.'

'Oh, yes?' I smiled to myself and wondered how many ghosts of his imprisoned ancestors still lingered in this old gaol? It wasn't a bad place to spend eternity, I decided. It was airy and surprisingly light once you came out of the dungeons. Then Beth gave a cute smile and filled her nappy. Any lingering ghosts bolted for cover.

'Apparently, the rest of the Charlton boys decided to come and break him out.' His voice rose with excitement.

'What happened?'

'When the gaolers heard that the Charltons had gathered to gallop into Hexham, they fled. They left the gaol unguarded and the reivers rescued Topping without a fight.'

'Lucky fellah.' I could see he liked this image of the Charlton men thundering into town to break into the gaol and save one of their own. *'We've come for our boy...'*

'It didn't end there. A few years later, they recaptured Topping and imprisoned him further away in Berwick castle which was then devastated by the plague. Everyone died except Topping.'

'How?'

'I don't know – it just says that he walked over the dead bodies of his gaolers and out of the open castle gate.'

'It sounds like he had the luck of the devil.'

'No, not the devil,' Chris declared, firmly. 'He's one of ours. He had 'the luck of the Charltons'.'

I smiled. Ever since Chris's grandfather survived all four years of WW1, his family believe they have a lucky streak.

Just before the museum shut, we clattered back down the wide, stone staircase to the gift shop.

Chris engaged the lady behind the counter in conversation and promptly informed her of our surname.

'Charltons, eh? Northumberland's full of 'em.' She giggled.

This made sense. Those six hundred men without horses must have had a hobby or two; breeding would probably have been one of them.

Still excited by all our discoveries, we chatted to her for a while about the museum. She helped us to choose a framed map of the Border region for a souvenir and asked us where we were staying.

'While you're up at Kielder, you ought to gan and take a look at Hesleyside.'

'What's that?' I asked.

'It's the famous site where the Charlton reivers would gather before they went onto plunder the Scots. It's bin the home of the leader of the Charlton tribe since the fourteenth century.'

Intrigued, Chris whipped out the maps the minute we arrived back at the car. I began to wonder if we would get to our B&B before dark.

'It's all right,' he reassured me. 'Look – Hesleyside Hall is on the way to Kielder.'

Fired up with enthusiasm about our ancestral heritage, we found the hall, pulled over and took a few photographs. Built in 1719, the present mansion at Hesleyside occupies the site of a fourteenth century Pele Tower.

Hesleyside Hall, Bellingham

According to the woman in the gift shop, there is a legend that the Charlton reivers would gather here for a drunken feast before they went out on a raid. When the pantry was empty, the lady of the house brought out a spur on a silver platter as a signal to the men to get on their 'hosses', set off for Scotland and fetch home the bacon, beef and mutton.

Smitten with the legend, Hesleyside and the whole Border Reiver heritage, Chris began to daydream he was the long-lost heir of Hesleyside. The romance of the history, the glorious fresh air and the excitement of our discoveries were a heady mixture.

Later that night, after an excellent meal in the pub and a several pints of Guinness, Chris became uncharacteristically bold.

'I think we'll return to Hesleyside tomorrow and drive up to the front door.'

I spluttered into my chardonnay.

'Sorry? What?'

'We'll go and introduce ourselves to the Charltons of Hesleyside.'

I stared at him in surprise, stunned by his announcement and slightly appalled by it at the same time. Quiet, polite and shy, Chris had never been prone to harassing total strangers in their own homes before. In fact, he would have made a lousy door-to-door salesman.

'And what'll we say to them, exactly?'

He thought for a moment, eyes misted with romance and Guinness.

'How about: 'We're here!'.'

Fortunately, he sobered up the next day and I persuaded him to leave the Charltons of Hesleyside undisturbed. We abandoned our surprise assault on the hall – for the time being.

This trip to the North Tyne valley inspired us.

Everywhere we turned, we found more information about the Charltons and the reiver heritage. By the time we left Northumberland in the summer of 1995, we were desperate to begin our family history research. We wanted to uncover characters like 'Topping' and links to Hesleyside and the Charlton reivers. But there were 500 years between us and them and we didn't have a clue where to start.

Our genealogical research has been a long journey. It has taken us nearly eighteen years to scrape away the fogs of time and inch back through the centuries to 1700. We are still a couple of centuries away from 'Topping Charlton' and I doubt that we'll ever manage to get our line back to the time of the reivers. Much to Chris's disappointment, I suspect that we'll never find the evidence to prove him the rightful heir to Hesleyside Hall.

Kielder Water, Northumberland

Yet, the stories we have uncovered are more fascinating, amusing and tragic than we could ever have imagined. We may not have Topping but we have our convict Jamie and his wife, Cilla. We have 'Soldier Will', the tragic Mary Famelton, 'Stationmaster Will' and a whole host of dysfunctional Charltons who lived at North Carter Moor farm in the 18th century. I suspect we have dug up enough excitement and salacious gossip to fill another series of historical novels, so perhaps we should be more satisfied.

This is our family history.

CHAPTER TWO
'Soldier Will' and the Floozy

Chris and I first met in Scarborough in 1986. At the time, we were both going out with other people. Our partners worked together and occasionally the four of us would 'double date'. Apart from his dodgy obsession with Middlesbrough Football Club, I thought Chris was a decent and very loyal guy. He had a great sense of humour and small children adored him.

A few years later, we were both single again and Chris began a concerted campaign to make me fall in love with him. He quickly discovered that the way to my heart was through food and he began to woo me with homemade spaghetti bolognaise. Surprisingly, it worked. There is something very attractive about a guy who you've known for ages, who likes small children and can rustle up a good spag bol.

Chris and Karen Charlton, May 1993

Despite a problem with the vicar who thought I was a bigamist, (don't ask – this story would fill another book) we married in May 1993. I worked from home as a freelance training officer for the health service at the time and travelled all over the country with my job. It made sense for me to leave my flat in Scarborough and move up the coast to Chris's home in Marske-by the-Sea.

I found myself instantly thrown into a large, confusing family of Charltons, Hammonds, Mentiers, McIntyres, Fords and Parks. Chris has ten first cousins, and dozens of other relatives, some of whom share the same first name. We tend to only meet up at weddings and funerals and I'm still not quite sure who is who.

His large family had lived in this area on the north-east coast of Yorkshire for over a century. Even after twenty years of marriage and life in Marske, I still feel like 'the new girl in town'. Occasionally, I crack a joke that I was imported to widen the gene pool. In the light of our subsequent discoveries about Northumberland's most notorious burglar, it is probably a good thing I did move north and do my bit to diffuse the hereditary criminal element.

Marske-by-the-Sea

Charlton was a familiar surname in the local community. Three generations had spawned Charlton cricket players, footballers, school masters and mistresses, plumbers, electricians, a florist shop and a taxi firm. In fact, when 15-year-old Chris started work at the Dorman Long steelworks in Lackenby, one of the questions they asked the terrified lad was:

'Are you one of the 'Marske' Charltons?'

When we began to research his ancestry, we began in the place where all genealogists usually start, with the family folklore and legend passed down through the ages. Here we were very lucky. Chris's relatives had plenty of information to tell us about the 20th century generations of the family.

In addition to this, one of Chris's great-uncles, Mervyn Charlton, had self-published a couple of short booklets about his childhood in the 1920s. *Sand in my Shoes* and *More Sand in my Shoes* are whimsical tales of Charlton family life and they proved invaluable in our research.

Books about Marske by James Mervyn Charlton

But the Marske Charltons were far from an 'ideal family' – our branch definitely had its flaws.

We already knew that Chris's distant ancestors came from County Durham and were employed in the booming Victorian railway industry. Allegedly, many of them worked as stationmasters. It was really hard to do much genealogical research back in 1994, before the online explosion of internet sites changed all our lives. So, we concentrated on building up a strong picture of the more recent generations. We tried to fill in the gaps about the Marske Charltons. We wanted to get a clearer picture of who they were, and where they had come from.

Chris's great-grandparents were John-George Charlton (1869 - 1936) and his wife, Phoebe Ann (neé Jacques.) They were the first Charltons to move to Marske. John-George worked as a rail freight manager in the smoggy, industrial 'Ironopolis' of Middlesbrough. Their older children were born in Middlesbrough and sadly, some of them died there too.

At the turn of the 20th century, Middlesbrough was the throbbing heart of Teesside's vibrant iron and steel industry. Noisy, dirty and dangerous, the god Vulcan reigned supreme and hammered out a ceaseless stream of metal, night and day from the roaring blast furnaces. Huge ladles of molten iron swayed precariously from the towering gantries. Above them, the angry sky glowed red. Cold winds howled down the Tees estuary and rocked the heavily-laden ships crammed in the docks.

Steam engines belched out filth and grime into the smog, strained against the weight of their load on railway lines which crisscrossed the 'wurks' like a spider's web. Behind the smoke-blackened window of his office, John-George coordinated this constant stream of rail traffic as it hauled away the precious metal which built the Sydney Harbour Bridge and other iconic monuments across the globe.

Meanwhile, his young children joined in with gangs of local youngsters to raid the mountains of dusty coke which lined the river bank and fed the insatiable appetite of an industry which never slept. They crawled on their bellies beneath perimeter fences, dodged blows from the muscled and tattooed arms of angry iron workers, and stole from the shimmering piles of fuel before racing back to their damp tenements and overcrowded terraced houses.

John-George & Phoebe Charlton

In 1908, John-George and Phoebe decided to take their young family to live in the cleaner air at the coast. The couple had already lost two children to diphtheria and pneumonia in Middlesbrough and they were concerned about the health and moral development of the rest. John-George bought a five-bedroomed house on the High Street known as Healam House. Marske is older than the Domesday Book but it had moved with the times. There were two railway stations in the village and he commuted back to work in Middlesbrough on the train.

Eight of their eleven children survived to adulthood.

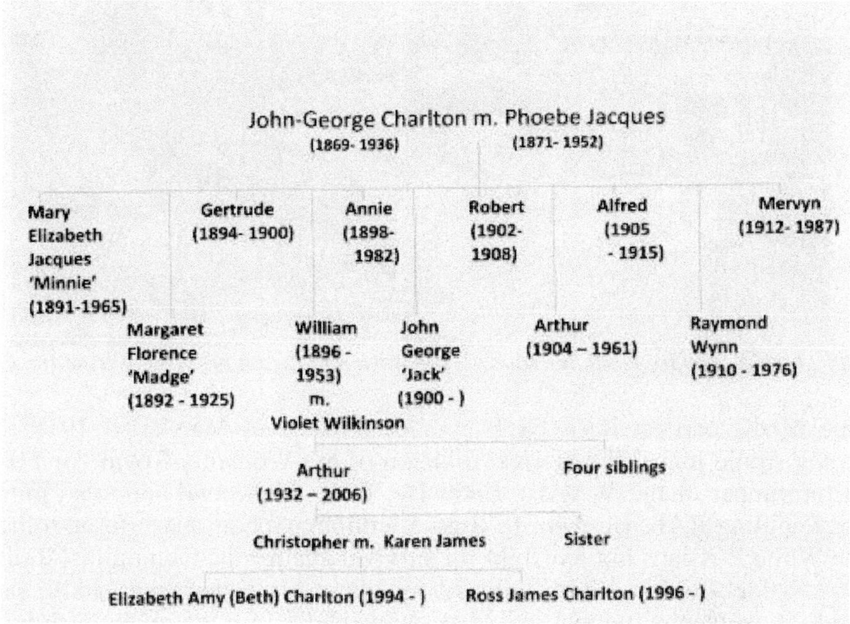

Uncle Mervyn's books tell us that he and his siblings enjoyed an idyllic childhood in this one-thousand-year-old fishing village. Theirs was now a more sedate world of cricket matches, golden beaches, barn dances and sing songs around the piano. It smelt of freshly-baked bread, brine and seaweed. The village resounded with the cries of seagulls, the crack of leather on willow and the gentle applause of spectators. The young Charltons stood on the sand dunes and watched fishing cobles ride the swell of the turning tide. They rolled hoops down the narrow, cobbled streets lined with white-washed cottages and hurled balls at the coconut shy in the village fête, where coloured bunting fluttered like ribbons in the breeze.

John-George and Phoebe's children thrived in this world, but even our forgotten corner of northern England did not remain untouched by the carnage of World War One. The suffering caused by the First World War affected every family in Britain, including ours.

Old Marske c. 1930. Healam House is the third terraced house along from the left.

One of the earliest RAF bases was established at Marske in 1918 and young Annie joined the clerical division of the Women's Royal Air Force (a forerunner of the WAAF). Likewise, Jack, the second son, also joined the fledgling RAF. He went to Russia with an expeditionary force to help the White Russians in their fight for survival against the Communist Reds.

Jack returned with wild stories about his experiences and a sack load of souvenirs which included snow shoes, fur gauntlets, yards of parachute silk and a collection of helmets. He told his family grim stories of the terrible conditions in Russia, where starving children scrambled for every morsel of food the RAF men could give them. He is remembered – along with his older brother, William – on a plaque of WW1 Servicemen in St. Mark's Church, Marske. Sadly, there is no plaque in the church to commemorate Annie's contribution to the war effort in WW1 or the hard work and dedication of the other women of Marske who joined the armed forces.

Jack and Annie in RAF uniform 1918

The other war hero of the family was Chris's grandfather, William Charlton. Ironically, he was also the embarrassing black sheep of the family, who scandalised the family with his fling with an older woman.

Born in 1896, Soldier Will's life was ruined by World War One. The carnage broke out in 1914 when he was eighteen years old and he signed up immediately. At first, he joined the Northumberland Fusiliers but later transferred to the newly-formed machine gun corps.

William's war, like many others, was spent mired in the trenches, constantly under fire, always at risk from a sniper or a shell. Shells could take out anyone, as William saw, when he watched one hit a runner who was taking messages between two British trenches. The shell blew off the poor man's head. The headless corpse continued to run on for several yards before it finally stumbled and fell to the ground.

On another occasion, William's platoon was trapped overnight in a shell hole. Darkness fell and it became impossible to see their hands in front of their faces. Amid all the slimy mud and gore around them, he felt a few blades of grass by his side. He hunkered down and spent most of that grim night nervously fingering the leaves of the plant. When dawn broke, he got a nasty shock. He had spent the night stroking the beard of a dead German soldier, whose decapitated head and chin poked up out of the mud.

'Soldier Will' (1896 - 1953)

Machine Gunners (WW1)

The trauma of his long exposure to the carnage and horror of WW1 never left William alone. Decades later, he would still wake up screaming with nightmares.

Wounded in 1918, during the Spring Offensive after Ypres, William suffered from his physical injuries for the rest of his life. Great-uncle Mervyn mentioned it in *Sand in my Shoes.* Mervyn was a very young child at the time so the full emotional significance of the *Missing in Action* telegram escaped him:

'William was reported missing after the Battle of Lys. Not that I knew any details of the event at the time. For three weeks, I noticed a strained air in the family. I did not feel it too deeply, not being fully aware of what it meant. I know that the family jumped for joy when one day a postcard arrived from him. It said briefly, in French, that he had been wounded and was in a French hospital...'

[Initially, the Charltons couldn't find anyone in Marske to translate the French into English.]

'...Later, when my brother was discharged from the army after the war, he told us the story of how he came to be wounded. After the Germans had broken through the British lines after the Second Battle of Lys, my brother, retreating with the others, took shelter with French troops in a cellar. A shell hit them and killed many but he and another British soldier were

badly wounded in the leg. However, he managed to crawl outside and get into a French ambulance which took him to a French dressing-station and then to Rouen Hospital. William's leg was badly shattered by shrapnel but after a rest, he went back to the front...'

Once the war finished, William found work as a plumber but his damaged leg troubled him for the rest of his life and he found it hard to work.

'I remember one day when William had to be brought from Marske railway station in a barrow pushed by a porter. Apparently, his leg had given way as he got out of the train on his way back from Middlesbrough, where he worked as a plumber on the ships being built in Smith's Docks. So, his wound was a telling one. He often suffered from it in later years...'

From *Sand in my Shoes* by James Mervyn Charlton

Uncle Mervyn also tells us that despite his injuries, the de-mobbed William was still a typical young man in every other way. A 'sharp dresser', he enjoyed a night out with his mates and chatted up the girls. He owned a fashionable silver-topped walking cane, which he needed to aid his mobility.

It must have been hard for William to adjust to the expectations and Edwardian values of his church-going, middle-class parents when he returned from the carnage of the Belgium trenches. He had gone away to war an innocent, eighteen-year-old boy and returned a damaged man, a witness to horrors his family could not begin to imagine. Resuming a village life of church fêtes, whist drives and cricket teas must have been difficult for him. In the war, he had lived every day as if it was his last and snatched fleeting moments of pleasure wherever he could find them.

This is probably why he became involved with Gertrude Riley from Scrafton Place. The surviving details of his affair with this woman are sketchy and Uncle Merv certainly never sullied his books by mentioning it, but we understand that William and Gertie had a passionate sexual relationship. Some members of the family think that Gertie was married and their relationship was adulterous; others say she was a war widow. What is clear, however, is that in a small village like Marske, where everyone knew everyone else and their business, they didn't stand a chance of keeping the affair private. Inevitably, William and Gertie's secret trysts soon became common knowledge.

William's parents were outraged when they found out their eldest son consorted with this floozy. According to family legend, his shocked mother sent him away to live with relatives in Leeds until the scandal died down.

After a year or two in the city, William moved on with his life. He met and married Violet Lilian Wilkinson, a young woman originally from Askrigg in Wensleydale. Their relationship seems to have healed the rift with his parents because they returned to Marske after their marriage in 1927 and their five children were brought up here.

Plagued with pain and hampered by his disability, William struggled to find and keep a job. They were always the poor branch of the family and lived in a two-bedroomed, terraced house, far too small to accommodate their growing brood. One of their four sons, my father-in-law, Arthur, gained a scholarship to the local grammar school but was forced to leave at sixteen because his parents needed him to earn his keep.

William died in 1953, aged fifty-seven, exactly twelve months before Chris was born. Although they never met, Chris hero-worships his soldier grandfather and a framed photograph of William hangs in our hallway. Chris has tried repeatedly to track down William's service record in The National Archives, but so far, he has been unsuccessful. Many official records from the Great War were destroyed by a German bomb which landed on the National Archives during the *Second* World War, and it seems likely that our William's records were among these.

Soldier Will may have died prematurely but we still believe he had 'the luck of the Charltons', the family lucky streak. We believe this because he managed to survive all four years as a soldier during WW1. This is an amazing achievement when you consider that thousands of men died within hours of arriving at the front line. The missing records mean it will always remain a mystery exactly *how* William managed to survive. But the fact remains that he *did*.

William stayed upwind of the deadly chlorine gas, dodged out of the way of lethal shells, bullets and shrapnel. He became an expert at keeping his head down. Somehow, against all the odds, he hung onto his sanity and was always in the right place at the right time. For this we salute him.

None of us would be here without that amazing ability to survive.

Mervyn, William and Ray Charlton 1916

CHAPTER THREE
Victorian Respectability?

When *FamilySearch* (the genealogy organisation established and run by The Church of Jesus Christ of Latter-day Saints) first opened their website in May 1999, Chris and I were two of the millions of amateur genealogists who logged onto the site and overloaded it. *FamilySearch.org* is one of the most heavily used genealogy sites on the Internet and has remained in my list of 'Favourites' ever since.

But I have to confess we first approached this website with ignorance and trepidation.

'When we register, do a crowd of Mormons suddenly appear at the front door with Bibles?' Chris joked.

His humour masked our nervousness about this new-fangled thing called the 'Internet' *and* The Church of Jesus Christ of Latter-day Saints.

'I don't understand,' I said. 'Why has an American religious sect gone to so much trouble with a load of old British documents?'

'It's not just us,' Chris informed me. 'They've spent sixty years microfilming genealogical records from all around the world.'

'Why? What exactly did they want from us and our ancestors?'

We hesitated and wondered. In the end, curiosity overcame our doubts and we typed 'John-George Charlton' into the search box for the 1881 British census. This was the first time a census document had been uploaded onto the Internet. We couldn't wait to see what it revealed.

Relatives had told us John-George originally came from County Durham and he claimed to have three brothers who were all stationmasters. But all of this remained hearsay, and up to 1999 we had been unable to trace our ancestors any further back than the family's arrival in Marske. We knew from his gravestone that John-George was born in 1869. By our calculations he should have been twelve years old in 1881 and still living with his unknown parents – he was.

John-George's parents were William and Margaret Charlton. This particular William – whom we quickly nicknamed 'Stationmaster Will' - ran the North Eastern Railway (NER) station in Stanhope in County Durham and lived at number 1, Station Terrace.

1981 CENSUS

Name	Age	Occupation	Place of Birth
William Charlton	45	Stationmaster	Elsdon, NBL
Margaret Charlton	49	Wife	Pensher, Co. Durham
Robert W. Charlton	15	Railway Clerk	Darlington, Co. Durham
Mary E. F. Charlton	14	Scholar	" "
John G. Charlton	12	"	" "
Alfred (twin) Charlton	7	"	" "
James (twin) Charlton	7	"	" "
Priscilla Charlton	6	"	" "
Annie Charlton	4	"	Stanhope, Co. Durham

We poured over every word in the document. We had a whole new generation of ancestors to explore and we lapped up every last detail.

They had moved around a lot. William originated from the tiny Northumberland village of Elsdon, whereas his slightly-older wife was from the small village of Penshaw in County Durham.

Most of the children were born in Darlington, a booming railway town in the nineteenth century. The birth of the youngest daughter, Annie, in Stanhope in 1877 suggested that the Charltons left Darlington and moved to Stanhope sometime between 1875 and 1877.

We needed to go back another ten years and find them in Darlington on the 1871 census but at this point in time none of the other censuses were online.

To find our family on the c.1871 meant a trip to the records office to trawl through microfilm spools – a process which has always made me very nauseous. In addition to this, record offices are joyless, quiet places, full of the ghosts of the ancestors and unsuitable play areas for their descendants. So, while we were still ~~hampered~~ blessed with two young children, we decided to leave the records office undisturbed and take the kids and the camera on some day trips to the places mentioned on the 1881 census.

Our first visit was to Stanhope and the family home in 1881. Station Terrace is only yards away from the railway station.

No. 1 Station Terrace, Stanhope

My own childhood was spent (or perhaps I should say, 'misspent?') trespassing on railway tracks and in engine sheds with my steam-engine-loving Dad. I had innocently absorbed a vast store of knowledge about freight trains at a young and tender age and it helped me to imagine the scene in mid-Victorian Stanhope. I could picture the powerful trains as they hauled their heavy loads up the incline of Weardale and belched black smoke over Margaret Charlton's clean laundry in the back yard of Station Terrace.

Another trip to Darlington Railway Museum brought us an incredible find. We stumbled across this wonderful photograph of Stanhope Railway Station.

The inscription on the back of the photograph simply reads: 'old platform at Stanhope circa 1893/4.' But we knew instantly that we had found a picture of William Charlton and possibly some of his sons.

William Charlton, his staff and sons on the 'old platform' at Stanhope

The white-haired man, third from the right, shared a strong family resemblance to Chris's father and our photographs of John-George. The white waistcoat also told us that this man held the status of the station master. But who were the other men and boys – especially the cocky beggar posing on the train?

Five years ago, we made contact with Chris's cousin, Jackie (daughter of Raymond Wynn Charlton) and we solved the mystery. Jackie owned another old family photograph of the Stanhope Charltons. When we cross-referenced the faces of men in the photograph, it became obvious that the poser on the train was eldest son, Robert. In addition to this, one of the younger men in the line-up was James, one of the twins.

Back row: Annie, James, unknown cousin, Mary and Robert Charlton. Seated: William and Margaret. Front row: Priscilla Charlton and two unknown cousins.

When we did eventually track down the Charltons on the 1871 census it threw up a few surprises. William and Margaret lived in a row of small terraced houses next to Darlington railway station and William worked as a railway warehouse foreman. We had expected this. The railway industry was Darlington's main source of employment in the 19th century and to become a stationmaster by 1881, William must have worked his way up through the ranks of the North Eastern Railway company.

What we didn't expect to find were two more sons, both of whom were left behind in Darlington when the rest of the family moved to Stanhope. Their eldest son, Arthur, was apprenticed to a blacksmith at the time of his father's promotion, so he had moved into lodgings to finish his apprenticeship. But sadly, William and Margaret also left behind another son – in a grave in Darlington's West Cemetery.

When we researched this child's short life, I felt pangs of grief for them all. Yes, they would have been excited when William achieved his promotion to stationmaster. The move meant more money, greater security, the larger house at Stanhope and better social standing.

But it also split up their family. It must have been heart-breaking to leave young Arthur behind in Darlington and be wrenched away from their infant's grave. Did Margaret worry about who would tend to it and visit it once they left town? I know that this would have bothered me.

Genealogy always starts off as a search for facts, dates, places and people but it often became an emotional journey – sometimes an emotional rollercoaster ride. Behind those impassive faces in the photographs and the black ink on the historical documents, lay human stories of pain, suffering, joy and elation, most of which we can only imagine.

The 1871 census gave us the complete picture of William and Margaret's offspring. In total they had nine children, eight of whom survived to adulthood.

Arthur Charlton	Born 1862, Newbottle.
Robert W. Charlton	Born c.1865, Darlington.
Mary E. F. Charlton	Born 1866, Darlington.
John George Charlton	Born August 19th, 1868 Belgrave Street, Darlington.
William Charlton	Born 1870. Died 1874 aged 3 ½ years. Buried Feb 3rd, 1874.
James & Alfred Charlton (twins)	Born 1873 Darlington.
Priscilla Charlton	Born 1874, Darlington.
Annie Charlton	Born 1877, Stanhope.

We decided to track down the marriage certificate of Station Master Will and Margaret. We sent for John-George's birth certificate to get his mother's maiden name and discovered it was 'Wynn'.

'That's the middle name of my Great-Uncle Raymond,' Chris noticed.

John-George had given us a clue to his mother's maiden name when he named one of his sons and we had ignored it. We later found out that 'Wynn' was also the middle name of William and Margaret's son, Robert. If we only we had paid greater attention to this family practice of passing down the maiden names, and paid for a more birth certificates, we could have saved ourselves years of frustration when our research hit a serious brick wall a few years later. But we didn't.

We began to search for a marriage certificate for a William Charlton and a Margaret Wynn. In light of Margaret's rampant fertility, it looked like she and William were married one or two years before Arthur's birth in 1862.

Simple.

No, it wasn't. Assuming anything in genealogy is a huge mistake. In William and Margaret's case, our mistake was to assume that because they were the epitome of Victorian respectability in later life, they had always conformed to the expectations of society when it came to marriage and children. They hadn't.

We couldn't find their marriage certificate where we expected it to be – in the years before Arthur's birth – because William and Margaret were not married when Arthur was born; he was illegitimate.

Born on May 11th, 1862 at Sunderland Street in Newbottle, Houghton-le-Spring, Margaret baptised her first son Arthur Charlton Wynn. His birth certificate describes him as the 'illegitimate son of Margaret Ann Wynn' but his paternity is clearly obvious from his middle name. I later found out that the local workhouse was situated on Sunderland Street and my internal alarm bells began to ring. Was Margaret incarcerated in the workhouse when she gave birth to Arthur? If so, why? What on earth had happened?

We finally discovered that William and Margaret were married two years **later** on May 22 nd, 1864, at St. Margaret's chapel in Durham. We have no idea why William and Margaret didn't get married until two years after the birth of their first son, Arthur Charlton Wynn.
Were they too poor to get married, perhaps? Did one of them refuse to marry the other? Had her furious father thrown out his unmarried and pregnant daughter and cast her upon the charity of the workhouse?

So many questions – with absolutely no answers. Some mysteries can never be solved. This is the problem with genealogical research; it often raises more questions than it answers.

St. Margaret's chapel, Durham.

Later, on the 1861 census we found William Charlton visiting the home of his future wife and her parents. It looks like he was courting Margaret back in 1861 but again, this is only speculation. What is clear, however, is that in 1861, before he impregnated their eldest daughter, the Wynn family welcomed Stationmaster Will into their family home.

1861 CENSUS

Name	Age	Occupation	Place of Birth
Robert Wynn	55	Grocer	Washington, Co. Durham
Elizabeth Wynn	50	Wife	Houghton-le-Spring, County Durham
Margaret Wynn	29	Dressmaker	Pensher, Co. Durham
George Wynn	26	Engine Fitter	Washington, Co. Durham
William Charlton	25	Porter	Elsdon, NBL

Despite all our efforts, we have never found out what happened in this three-year period (1861-1864) in the lives of Margaret and William. Nothing has been passed down through the generations in family folklore and no historical records remain to give us a clue. Margaret and William took the secrets of this difficult patch in their relationship to their graves; they were probably grateful to move on with their lives and forget about their early problems.

CHAPTER FOUR
The Weardale Railway

Between 1832 and 1834, the Stanhope and Tyne railway was built. Thirty-three miles long, it connected the mineral rich crags above Stanhope with the Tyneside docks at South Shields. At its peak in the 1870s, ten passenger trains a day and one hundred freight trains a week thundered up and down the line. That's one heck of a lot of trains belching out steam and coal dust to land on Margaret Charlton's laundry.

The station at Stanhope was at the end of the line until its controversial expansion up to Wearhead in 1893.

On October 21nd, 1893, Sir Joseph Whitwell Pease, deputy chairman of the NER, ceremoniously cut the first sod for the nine-mile extension from Stanhope. According to local newspaper, *The Northern Echo*, this was a day *'which has long been looked forward to with pleasurable anticipation'*.

They erected a grandstand so the crowds could watch the ceremony; brass bands played, and as Sir Joseph slid his inscribed, silver spade with its ebony shaft into the turf, the Allendale and Stanhope Volunteers fired rifle shots to announce the news to the world.

'He cut the first sod, shovelled it into the barrow and wheeled it along a plank, depositing the sod and returning with the barrow in quite a workmanlike manner, to the amusement and admiration of the assembly,' wrote the *Echo*.

I have often wondered what our stationmaster and his sons were doing on this day. Did William leave his lads to run the station, join the crowd and watch Sir Joseph wield his silver spade?

Great festivities followed the sod-cutting. About 700 children from the four schools between Westgate and Lanehead each received a free tea and a commemorative medal. Punch and Judy shows, balloon ascents *'and a grand display of fireworks'* entertained the crowds. Did Margaret and her three daughters put on their best clothes and hats and take a seat in the grandstand to watch the fun? Or as the wife and daughters of an NER Stationmaster, were they roped in to serve the teas for the 700 children?

But the celebrations for the new stretch of railway line soon turned sour. The NER employed a firm of cheap contractors from Croydon to do much of the work – a move bitterly resented by the large army of unemployed, northern dales men.

Then a Weardale winter struck. Thirteen weeks of continuous snow followed and progress was delayed by incidents in which four workmen died. How much stress this caused our William during the two years of the extension's construction, or how much it hastened his early death, we shall never know. There is no doubt in my mind that the expansion of the railway line affected him badly. As the new rail line reached out its iron tentacles from his station at Stanhope into the rugged landscape of Weardale, William would have been unable to escape the politics, the change, the strife and the pressure which went with this development. For a start, Stanhope railway station also got a new layout and platform.

Stanhope Railway Station 1895. How many of those porters are Charltons, I wonder?

On October 21st, 1895 Sir Joseph returned, in *'a terribly depressing downpour of rain'*, to formally open the line extension. Nearly 400 people climbed aboard the first train from Stanhope to Wearhead and hundreds more gathered in the downpour to witness the proceedings. Events like this clearly attracted a lot of attention. It is poignant to recognise that, just as hundreds have recently gathered in the rain to watch the Olympic torch pass through the North East, regional pride was as strong then as it is now.

When we read the *Echo's* detailed reports of the ceremony, we learnt speaker after speaker repeated the phrase that the Weardale Railway was a *'legitimate enterprise'*. It sounds like everyone was trying to convince themselves.

At the sod-cutting, a lone voice wondered whether the NER had *'ventured too far?'* History suggests that this extension was, indeed, a venture too far.

T. E. Routhwaite in his 1965 book *The Railways of Weardale* says:

'Regrettably, the extension had come ten years too late, the great revival failed to materialise and apart from bursts of activity connected with the two world wars, the mining and quarrying gradually subsided so that the extension to Wearhead never carried the weight of traffic that had been forecast.'

The Weardale Railway line finally closed in the 1960s.

1896 – A BLEAK YEAR

On February 6th, 1896, barely six months after the completion of the extension of the railway line to Weardale, William Charlton died in Stanhope aged 60. His death certificate says he died of a heart attack and the burial register for Stanhope tells us he died 'at work'. The problems and extra work caused by the line expansion may have hastened his death.

On Tuesday February 11th, *The Northern Echo* gave an account of William's funeral:

INTERNMENT OF THE STANHOPE STATIONMASTER

'On Monday afternoon, the remains of the late Wm. Charlton, stationmaster at Stanhope over 20 years, were interred at Stanhope Cemetery amid every token of respect. The Bishop of Richmond performed the last sad rites, and gave a nice address in church to the bereaved friends. Miss Pulleine played the "Dead March" on the organ. A number of railway officials and workmen followed the deceased to his last resting place.'

William's grave is in the 'Old Cemetery' in Stanhope. All in all, we think this obituary is a moving tribute to a hard-working member of the local community and a highly-respected employee of the North Eastern Railway company. Of course, we now know William was also the grandson of a transported felon. But shush – don't tell the Bishop.

Two weeks later, in Middlesbrough, our ancestors John-George and Phoebe Charlton had their first son. They named him WILLIAM after his grandfather. A month after 'Stationmaster Will' left this Earth, 'Soldier Will' arrived.

The grave of William, Margaret and Priscilla Charlton

Tragically, six months after the death of William, Margaret Charlton also had to bury Priscilla, their second daughter. Aged only twenty-two, Priscilla died on November 4th, 1896.

Priscilla (Cilla) Charlton (1874 - 1896)

'We've got to find the other stationmasters,' Chris announced. 'Don't you remember? My Dad told us John-George had three brothers who worked as stationmasters – just like William.'

From the 1911 census, we discovered that the eldest two sons of this generation, Arthur (48) and Robert (45) were both still unmarried – and more significantly, childless – in 1911. Arthur had moved to Leeds and worked as a blacksmith's striker. Robert worked as a relief stationmaster at Frosterley station, near Stanhope.

'This is great!' Chris exclaimed in delight. He had always held a strong belief in primogeniture. 'Not only have we found one of the stationmaster brothers – but this also means that I am still in line to inherit the Charlton family pile. Any inheritance will come down the line through John-George, Soldier Will and my dad to me. I'm the eldest surviving great-great grandson of Stationmaster William Charlton.'

'Still got your sights set on Hesleyside, pet?' I smiled.

His eyes glazed over as he stared dreamily across the kitchen.

Robert Charlton (1866 -)

We had found one of the Charltons' legendary trio of station masters. But where were the remaining two brothers and what did they do for a living?

It didn't take us long to find out.

The 1911 census also revealed that one of the twins, Alfred, worked as the stationmaster in Danby, North Yorkshire, a mere ten miles away from our branch of the family in Marske. Strike two.

This only left Alfred's twin brother, James, to research. What happened to him?

We found James living in Leeds, where he worked as a 'clerk'. It doesn't specifically say *railway clerk* on the census but I would put money on it that James was a *railway clerk.* Like all William's sons, he had been brought up within yards of the North Eastern Railway and had worked for the company since he left school.

Unfortunately, we will have to wait until the 1921 census is released in the UK to find out if James also got promoted and followed in the footsteps of his father and older brothers to the stationmaster's office. I have a strong suspicion that he did.

Victorian respectability? Well, the Bishop of Richmond who spoke at William's funeral obviously thought so or he wouldn't have attended…

…but little did he know about the scandal in the generations before.

James Charlton (1875 -)

CHAPTER FIVE
The Corbridge Charltons

To take the Charlton family further back than the 1861 census proved a real headache. From the c.1881, we knew that Stationmaster Will had been born in Elsdon, Northumberland in 1835.

Name	Age	Occupation	Place of Birth
William Charlton	45	Stationmaster	Elsdon, NBL

Unfortunately, we had an empty gap in his life between his birth in 1835 in Northumberland and the 1861 census, when he turned up in County Durham as a guest in the home of his future wife.

However, we did track down William's baptism entry in the church registers at Northumberland's record office.

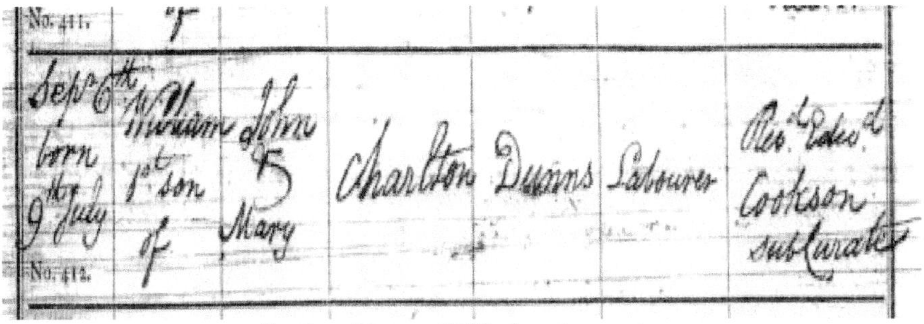
No. 411.
Sept 6th born 9th July
William 1st son of
John & Mary
Charlton
Duns
Labourer
Revd Edwd Cookson Sub Curate
No. 412.

Station Master Will's baptism entry

William's parents were John and Mary. We later discovered that John was the eldest son of Jamie Charlton, our family convict. Those of you who have already read *Catching the Eagle*, will recognise John as 'Jack', the young boy who develops an unusual friendship with a golden eagle.

At this point in our research, Chris was particularly pleased to see William described as the '1st son' of John and Mary Charlton. His claim to be the natural heir to any long-lost fortune remained undisputed; we had taken his family line back nearly two hundred years and he continued to be the oldest surviving Charlton son for five generations. Our claim on the Charlton pile (when we uncovered it) would be a legitimate one.

However, the arrival of William's baptism record heralded the arrival of a long, frustrating period when we struggled to find out any more information about William's parents or the gap in our knowledge between 1835 and 1861. In genealogy terms, problems like this are known as 'brick walls'.

We wrote more letters to the records office and asked if John and Mary had borne any more children in Elsdon? They had not. We visited Elsdon and examined the graves in the churchyard for clues. There were none.

St. Cuthbert's church, Elsdon

There were hundreds of John Charltons alive in the north-east of England in the nineteenth century. Dozens of them had wives called Mary and some had fifteen-year-old sons called William. Unfortunately, we just didn't know where to look next. Either William was that rare thing in Victorian England – an only child – or the family left Elsdon soon after William's birth.

We still went on short breaks to Northumberland with our children (who became surprisingly difficult and awkward about graveyard tours) and we wandered around the beautiful countryside searching for inspiration.

On one famous occasion, we decided to drive past 'Dunns' (the birthplace of William) for a nosey. It was the summer of 2001, the peak of the foot-and-mouth disease outbreak in the UK, and the wrong time in history to go traipsing around rural England. Undeterred, we checked out the map and found 'Dunns Farm', an isolated spot on the winding road between Elsdon and Rothbury.

It was a beautiful day and the farm was incredibly remote. The empty road unfurled through the rolling purple moorland like a silver ribbon. Our open windows emphasised the near-silence of the rural landscape around us. The forced mass-slaughter of Britain's livestock had left the countryside strangely quiet. Undisturbed by grazing sheep and lambs, the heather exploded into a violet and amethyst quilt across the hills. Rare plants like Juniper and dwarf cornel poked tender shoots nervously out of the scrub and swayed in the breeze beside the ferns and rye grass.

Set back from the road, Dunns Farm lay down a narrow meandering farm track. When we drove towards the entrance of this lane, we noticed that they had a sign advertising 'Bed and Breakfast' accommodation.

Chris flicked on the indicator and turned the car off the road and up the narrow farm track.

'What are you doing?' I gasped, as we bounced along from rut to rut.

'Let's be cheeky,' he said. 'We can knock on the door and ask to view the B&B accommodation. Tell them we intend to return to Northumberland in a few months' time and need somewhere to stay for this next trip.'

I was appalled. Memories of the night he suggested we stormed the privacy of Hesleyside Hall flooded back. Unfortunately, this time he was both sober and determined; there would be no U-turn on this narrow farm track. I slumped down in my seat and steeled myself to act the part. Years of marriage to Chris had fine-tuned my instincts; I knew when 'we' meant 'me'.

True to form, after we pulled up, Chris calmly got out of the car and began to fuss with the children. I was left to explain to the startled farmer and his wife why we needed to view their B&B accommodation.

They accepted my story without comment, welcomed us into their rambling Jacobean farmhouse and gave us a guided tour of the entire building. When we stood on the uneven floor in the centre of the old, low-beamed kitchen, Chris suddenly shivered.

'I can feel him,' he blurted out. 'My ancestor lived here. I've got chills running up my spine.'

The children and I were startled but impressed. So were the farmer and his wife, even though they hadn't a clue what he was talking about. I closed my gaping mouth, grabbed a child in each hand and began to back towards the door. We beat a hasty retreat.

The irony of this delightful little story is that we were completely in the wrong place.

Years later, we discovered that William was born at *Dunns Houses* to the east of Elsdon – not *Dunns Farm*. I have often teased Chris about his 'spine-shivering' experience. I wasn't prepared to let him get away lightly after he forced me to tell a pack of lies to that lovely couple at Dunns Farm.

Dunns Houses. The real birthplace of 'Stationmaster Will' in 1835.

We finally solved the problem of our missing family in 2004. One night, as I flicked through *More Sand in my Shoes,* I spotted a sentence in the final chapter of the book which I had missed before:

'My father's origins were in Corbridge, Northumberland, where there are many Charltons in the local churchyard...'

I could have kicked myself for not being more thorough but we were delighted. I sent off for a microfiche of the index of the 1851 census for Corbridge and when it arrived, I hurried down to Marske library to use one of their microfiche readers. Fighting back the wave of nausea, I gritted my teeth and concentrated.

It was only an index but I knew immediately that I had found our family. They lived on the Main Street in Corbridge:

'Priscilla Charlton 74, John 47, Isabella 30, Mary 28, William 15, and James 11.'

From this list, I could see our fifteen-year-old William Charlton living with his father, John. There was also a woman called Mary in the house. Unfortunately, at twenty-eight years old she was far too young to have been William's mother. But what clinched this entry for me was the inclusion in the household of another woman called *Priscilla.*

Priscilla is a biblical name and is very rare in the UK but it wasn't unusual in our family. We already knew about another Priscilla (Stationmaster Will's daughter) who died tragically young in 1896. It now looked like we had found the poor girl's great-grandmother.

Convinced that these Charltons on the index belonged to us, I raced back home to my computer, logged on and asked another member of *ancestry.com* to do a 'look-up' for me on her copy of the 1851 census so I could see the household in more detail.

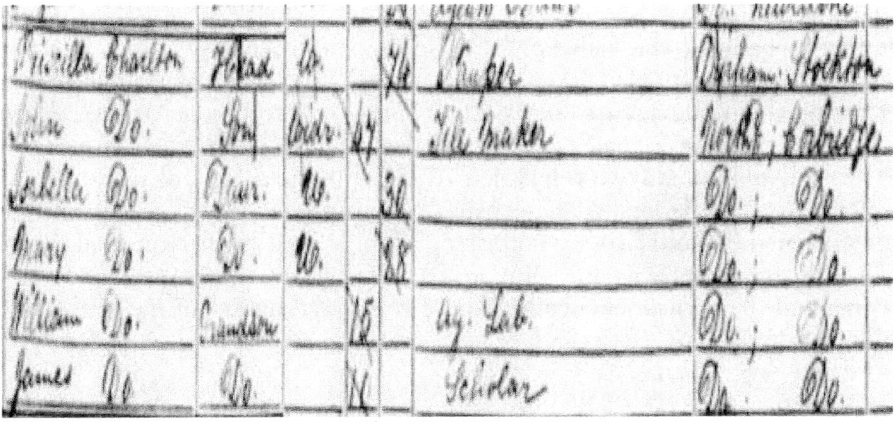

The 1851 Census

1851 Census
Main Street, Corbridge

Name	Age			Place of Birth
Priscilla Charlton	74	Head	Widow	Stockton, Co. Dur
John Charlton	47	Son	Widow	Corbridge NBL.
Isabella Charlton	30	Daur.		Corbridge NBL
Mary Charlton	28	Daur.		Corbridge NBL
William Charlton	15	Grand -son		Agric. Labourer Elsdon NBL
James Charlton	11	Grand -son		Corbridge NBL Student

In 1851, Priscilla Charlton lived with her son, John, her two daughters, and two grandsons. One of these young boys was our Stationmaster Will. We could see that forty-seven-year-old John was a widower; his wife Mary must have died.

Thanks to the inclusion of Priscilla on the census, we now had *two* new generations of the family to research. After years of stagnation we were on the move again. August 2004 turned out to be one of the busiest and most productive spates of genealogical research we ever undertook.

The kind lady who had helped me with the c.1851 also had access to the Northumberland 1841 census. A few hours later she sent me the details of our family (who, surprisingly, still lived at the same address). The 1841 census was the first to be carried out in the UK and only contained the names, occupation and a rough estimation of the age of the population.

1841 Census – HO107/838 – 04
Main Street, Corbridge

John Charlton	35	Labourer
John Charlton	14	Labourer
William Charlton	5	
Bell	25	Ag. Labourer
James	2	

We had found our William, now aged five and living with his father. We felt an incredible sense of satisfaction; we had finally traced Stationmaster Will back through *all* of the nineteenth century censuses.

The name 'Bell' confused us at first but we quickly worked out this was probably 'Belle' or 'Bella' – an abbreviation of Isabella, the name of John's sister.

Two unknown boys also lived in the household. James Charlton may have been William's younger brother but the fourteen-year-old boy called John Charlton was a mystery. Our William had been described on his baptism entry as 'The 1st son' of John and Mary Charlton, so this older lad called John couldn't be William's brother. But who was he?

Again, there was no sign of William's mother, Mary. Had she already died by 1841?

We decided it was time to put our hands in our pockets and fork out cash for some birth and death certificates.

CHAPTER SIX
1838: A Double Tragedy

It took us quite a while to unravel the relationships between the different Charltons we discovered on the earliest two censuses. Our research at this point went down three different tracks.

We wanted to know about the two mysterious boys, John and James, whom we had discovered in the household on the 1841 census. We wanted to know what had happened to John's wife, Mary, and we decided to see if Stationmaster Will had left us any other clues about his ancestors when he named his children. The surprise discovery of another 'Priscilla' in the family had set us thinking.

Young James turned out to be William's cousin, not his brother. His birth certificate told us that James was the illegitimate son of Isabella, John's unmarried sister. It seems that marrying the fathers of their children wasn't high on the priority list of the early-Victorian Charlton women. But at least they were a law-abiding bunch, who always registered the birth of their illegitimate progeny.

After his wife died, John Charlton invited Isabella and her small son to share his home and to help take care of his own, motherless son. Our earlier suspicions had been correct; Stationmaster Will was that rare thing in Victorian England – an only child. The two young lads were probably brought up like brothers.

Our rekindled interest in the names of Stationmaster Will's children also bore fruit. The surprise discovery of two Priscillas in our lineage suggested a pattern, or at least an occasional habit, of passing down family names through the generations. Had William Charlton left us any more clues in the names of his children? Had we missed anything else? Yes, we had.

We went back to the 1881 census and the middle initials of William's eldest daughter, Mary, now stood out like a beacon:

Mary E. F. Charlton.

Neither of her sisters possessed middle names, nor did the three younger brothers. What did her initials stand for?

We sent for her birth certificate and found out that her full name was *Mary Elizabeth Famelton Charlton.*

Famelton was – and still is – an unusual British surname. Just like 'Wynn', it is another maiden name brought into the family by one of the Charlton wives. Armed with this maiden name, it did not take us long to track down the banns record for a marriage between John Charlton and Mary.

On Jan 4th 1834
John Charleton of Corbridge Parish married Mary Famelton of Dunns Houses, Elsdon Parish at St. Cuthbert's Church, Elsdon.

Despite the misspelt surname, the mentions of *Dunns Houses* confirmed it. We had finally found a record of John and Mary's wedding. This episode taught us that we could not afford to overlook *anything;* a clue to Mary's maiden name had been staring us in the face since 1999 when we first logged onto *FamilySearch* and called up the 1881 census.

This also helped us to uncover the mystery of the older boy called John who lived with the family in 1841. I posted our discovery about John Charlton and Mary Famelton on a genealogy message board. A few days later, another member contacted me and told me that Mary Charlton (neé Famelton) was mentioned in the baptism register of neighbouring parish, Simonburn. We often find in the spellings are inconsistent in these old documents, but this is definitely our family.

On April 13th, 1834
John Fammelton, illegitimate son of Mary of Duns Houses, Parish of Elsdon, was baptised at St. Mungo's, Simonburn. (From IGI)

This explained the mysterious boy on the 1841 census. Fourteen-year-old John was Mary's illegitimate son from a previous relationship. She would have only been about fifteen when she gave birth to him, so perhaps 'previous relationship' is a bit of a euphemism. John Famelton would have been about six or seven years old when Mary married our John Charlton. We still have no idea why she waited all those years before she had her eldest boy baptised, or why only a few months after marrying John in Elsdon, they used the Simonburn church for the baptism. Had they moved village? We can only speculate that young John's sudden baptism had something to do with Mary's marriage. Perhaps her new husband or the vicar had insisted upon it?

One thing we are sure about though is that this young lad was not the natural son of our John Charlton. The vicar's statement in the baptism register that William was the *1st son* of John and Mary, seems very definite. Chris breathed a sigh of relief; our claim to the Charlton 'family pile' (when we found it) remained undisputed.

St. Mungo's Church, Simonburn

We now needed to find out what happened to Mary Charlton (neé Famelton).

We discovered that three different 'Mary Charltons' had died in Corbridge in the four years between the compulsory registration of births, deaths and marriages began in 1837 and the 1841 census. This seemed to be the place to start, so we sent off for all three death certificates for these 'Marys' in the hope that at least one of these women was our ancestor.

I can vividly remember the day they arrived. I had just cleaned the kitchen and was humming along tunelessly with radio when the post dropped on the doormat. I took the envelopes to the gleaming kitchen worktop, turned off the radio and slit them open with a knife.

The first death certificate wasn't ours, so I discarded it and turned my attention to the second.

I had found our Mary.

June 2nd 1838
Death of Mary Charlton aged 26 at Main St., Corbridge from Consumption. (Mother-in-law, Priscilla Charlton, present at death.)

A wave of sadness engulfed me. Mary was only been twenty-six years old when she died from tuberculosis. She had been married for a mere four years and left behind two young sons. Our family must have been devastated. Somehow that stark certificate really brought home to me the misery they must have suffered.

Unfortunately, there was worse to come.

Upset and thoughtful, I left the third death certificate untouched on the kitchen side for a while and made myself a cup of coffee. I had found our Mary and did not expect this last certificate to be relevant. However, curiosity always gets the better of me and eventually, I opened it. I was shocked to see it bore the same address.

Aug 22nd, 1838
Death of Mary Ann Charlton aged 13 weeks at Main St., Corbridge from Consumption.

I clutched the kitchen worktop to steady myself from the shock.

'Oh, no,' I groaned. 'No, no, no.'

Mary Charlton (neé Famelton) was pregnant with another child when she contracted consumption; she gave the disease to her baby daughter. We later discovered that little Mary Ann was born in May 1838.

For John Charlton, it must have been horrific. First, he saw his young wife waste away in front of his eyes. Then he watched helplessly as their baby daughter died from the same horrible disease a few weeks later. By August of 1838, the heartbroken man was alone with a three-year-old toddler, William, and his eleven-year-old stepson, John Famelton. I found this episode in our genealogical research quite upsetting and I am glad that John had his sister and mother to support him at this difficult time.

The family tree for this generation of Charltons was complete. It is more complicated than the other generations we have researched, but at least we finally know the relationships between all the people on the 1841 and 1851 censuses.

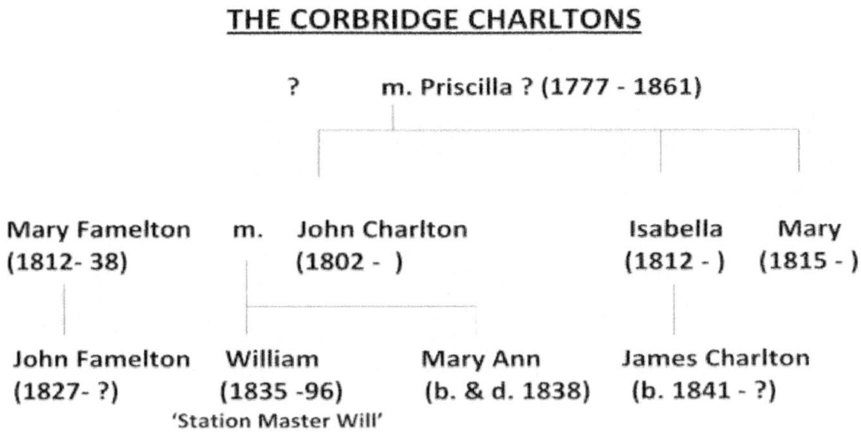

The Corbridge Charltons

John Charlton: 'The father-figure'

We now know that John was only eight years-old when his father, Jamie, was convicted for stealing the rent money from Kirkley Hall in Ponteland. This event must have been devastating for him, his mother and younger siblings. Already poverty-stricken, the records suggest that Priscilla had to rely on the charity of Heddon poor house to survive.

Two years later, Jamie left his prison cell in Northumberland for transportation to Australia. This was probably the last time John ever saw his father. In *Catching the Eagle*, I portrayed John (nicknamed 'Jack') as a quiet, bookish child who rescues the stray eagle from a trap and befriends it. I enjoyed creating his character and he quickly became one of my favourites.

Back in the real world, it seems that after those traumatic early years when he saw his father arrested and convicted, John Charlton's life became more humdrum. We can see from the censuses that he worked as an agricultural labourer on local farms or at the Corbridge tile works and pottery. Now that we had found him in 1841 and 1851 it was easy to locate him on the later censuses. We discovered that he lived with sister, Isabella, on Main Street in Corbridge for over thirty years; they still resided at the same address in 1861 and 1871. I suspect John never quite got over the death of his young wife, Mary. He never remarried and Isabella remained as his housekeeper until the end of their lives. Brother and sister grew old together.

The Charlton home (1838 - 1871) Main Street, Corbridge

Chris began to smirk when we took this photograph of John Charlton's home.

'You can see why he never moved house in thirty years,' he said.

'Why?'

'Look at what's behind us.'

I glanced round and realised we were standing next to the creamy, stone walls of the bustling Angel Inn, one of the oldest and most popular taverns in Corbridge. The pub is directly opposite John Charlton's cottage.

'It's every man's dream to live across the road from a pub,' Chris said. 'No wonder he didn't move.'

'Well, it certainly wouldn't have taken him long to stagger back home,' I conceded.

We have no evidence to show that John Charlton shared the well-documented drinking habits of his father, Jamie, but if he did then he was ideally situated for a night out, or two.

Corbridge pottery and tile works 1904

In 1851, John worked in as a tile maker at Walker's pottery in Corbridge. It's now a scheduled ancient monument and is in the care of English Heritage. It operated from the early 19th century until about 1914, producing pipes, tiles and low-grade pottery for agricultural use, as well as bricks.

By 1861, John had left the tile works and was employed as an agricultural labourer. The census for this year shows us that John and Isabella were now sharing their home with a nephew called James

Thompson. We later found out that they had another sister called Ann. James Thompson was her son. Both his parents were dead by 1861 and John and Isabella had offered their orphaned nephew a home.

1861 Census – RG9 3858
Main Street, Corbridge

John Charlton	Head	56	Ag. Lab	Milburn, Ponteland
Isabella Charlton	Sister	40	House-keeper	Milburn, Ponteland
James Thompson	Nephew	20	Tailor	Slaley, NBL

Despite help from a professional researcher, we have never tracked down what ultimately happened to John and Isabella; we don't know when or where they died. However, we do know that John was still alive in 1871 which makes him nearly seventy years old. He lived longer than his son, grandson and great-grandson.

The harsh justice of Jamie's conviction left Priscilla alone and destitute with five young children. As their eldest child – and a boy – John would have had to grow up quickly and take on a lot of responsibility for his mother and his younger siblings. The records show that he rose to the challenge. We can see from the census documents that he opened his home to the women in his family if they needed a roof over their heads and he became the 'father-figure' to four boys, three of whom were not his sons:

John Famelton – Mary Famelton's illegitimate son;
William Charlton – his son, our ancestor;
James Charlton – Isabella's illegitimate son, and
James Thompson – his sister Ann's son.

I imagine John to have been a caring person with a big heart and great love for children. I am still very moved by the sad loss of his wife and daughter and for these reasons he has become one of my favourite ancestors.

There are no photographs, of course, but in my mind, he is a large, cuddly man with a pack of small boys clambering all over him. I imagine that young children adored him, just like they adore my Chris. Although, we have no idea when John died, he lived long enough to see the birth of his first four grandchildren, the eldest children of Stationmaster Will.

Somehow, I get the impression that this would have delighted him.

CHAPTER SEVEN

'Husband Transported'

We turned back to the *FamilySearch* website to try to discover details about John's baptism and the name of Priscilla (Cilla's) husband. Thanks to her unusual first name we found it easily. John had been baptised at St Mary's church in Ponteland.

Search Results—FamilySearch.org — Free Family History and Genealogy Records

England Births and Christenings, 1538-1975: Priscilla Nimmo

No image available

Name:	John Charlton
Gender:	Male
Baptism/Christening Date:	26 Sep 1802
Baptism/Christening Place:	PONTELAND,NORTHUMBERLAND,ENGLAND
Birth Date:	04 Apr 1802
Birthplace:	
Death Date:	
Name Note:	
Race:	
Father's Name:	James Charlton
Father's Birthplace:	
Father's Age:	
Mother's Name:	Priscilla Nimmo
Mother's Birthplace:	
Mother's Age:	
Indexing Project (Batch) Number:	P00441-1
System Origin:	England-ODM
Source Film Number:	94975
Reference Number:	

John Charlton's baptism details

John's father was called James. (We later found out that James and Priscilla abbreviated their names to Jamie and Cilla.) We soon found the banns for Jamie's marriage to Priscilla Nimmo at Stamfordham church in 1800, but we could not find out anything else about this mysterious ancestor. Official records begin to peter out once you leave the Victorian era and hit the Regency period. The only things left to research are church records for baptisms, marriages and burials.

The 1851 census describes Cilla as a widow, but we couldn't find any burial records for our James Charlton in Corbridge or Ponteland. Either we were missing something significant, or Cilla had buried him in the back garden.

Then, in August 2004, we had an amazing piece of luck and made the discovery which would change our lives.

I was chatting on the message board again with that wonderful and very helpful man who had solved the riddle of the young John Famelton on the c.1841. I told him about Priscilla Charlton and her mysterious husband, James Charlton.

He replied that he had found a mention of a Priscilla Charlton in a Heddon Church register. She gave birth to an illegitimate daughter in 1815. In the baptism register, the vicar described her as a 'married woman' but then added that her husband was 'transported.'

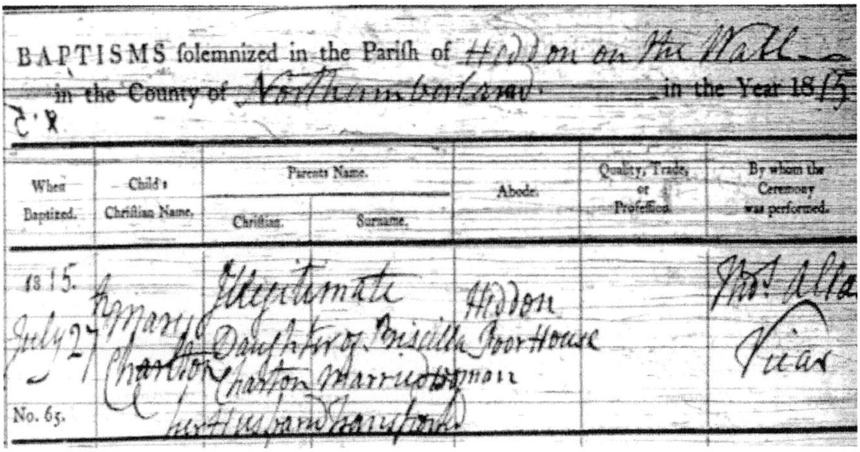
BAPTISMS solemnized in the Parish of Heddon on the Wall in the County of Northumberland in the Year 1815

When Baptized.	Child's Christian Name.	Parents Name. Christian.	Surname.	Abode.	Quality, Trade, or Profession.	By whom the Ceremony was performed.
1815. July 27 No. 65.	Mary Charlton	Illegitimate Daughter of Priscilla Charlton Married woman her Husband transported		Heddon Poor House		Vicar

'Husband transported'

I blinked, stared at the computer screen in surprise and burst out laughing. I could hardly speak.

'Chris!' I eventually gasped. 'You'd better come into the study – we've just found out what happened to your four times great-granddad!'

Reluctantly, he dragged himself away from the sport on TV and joined me in the small room we use as a study. While he glared at the computer screen, I continued to giggle my head off and helped myself to a large Barcadi with just a sniff of coke.

'My Grandma Gladys said you were a 'wrong 'un'. The old lady was right.'

'What is it?' He frowned. 'More illegitimacy?'

'Yes, and no. Look closer.'

Silently, he read the message. It was a while before he was able to comprehend this latest development.

'You always said you wanted to find links with those thieving thugs, the Border Reivers,' I smirked. 'Well, you're a step nearer. You've got your very own Regency criminal – we've a Regency reiver in the family.'

He muttered an unprintable expletive.

'Transported from Northumberland?' he demanded. 'Why? What did he do?'

'Dunno. We'll have to try and find out but it's bound to be bad. Transportation was a severe punishment.'

He shook his head in disbelief and swore again.

'My husband and children are descended from a convicted criminal,' I giggled. 'You're a right load of villains, the whole lot of you.'

'Stop laughing. It's not funny. He's obviously been framed.'

'What? Why?'

'Well, he's a Charlton – one of *our* Charltons.'

I stared at him in surprise but clamped my open mouth shut before I dribbled Bacardi down my chin. This probably wasn't the time to point out the illogical nature of that last remark. For a man desperate to trace his ancestry back to the Border Reivers, he looked quite miffed now a Regency jailbird had fallen out of his family tree.

'Have you tried to 'Google' James Charlton/ convict?' he asked.

'You're joking, right?'

'No, I'm serious. Try it.'

I shrugged and sat down at the computer. Chris and I may be a couple of amateurs, but we are *optimistic* amateurs.

I can't remember exactly which words I used to 'Google', probably something like *James/ Charlton/convict/Northumberland.* Surprisingly, it paid off.

We found an article about James Charlton under 'Victorian Mysteries' on a site called *Wearside Online:*

http://www.wearsideonline.com/liberty_is_sweet.html

Of course, Ponteland is on Tyneside (not Wearside) and the burglary happened in the Regency period (not the Victorian) and as we later discovered there are plenty more inaccuracies in this article, but it is still worth reproducing.

'Liberty is sweet

Wealthy landowner, Nathanial Ogle, owned Kirkley Hall, a farming estate just outside Ponteland in Northumberland. (He also owned other properties around the country.) The families who lived on his estate at Kirkley Hall always paid their rent on time and in the spring of 1809 it was time for the farmers and labourers to pay their half-yearly rent again. When he left his estate, Nathanial would leave Michael Aynsley, the owner of a nearby modest estate at Newham, in charge of his financial affairs; this time it was to collect the rents. Because of an increase, the rents would total £1,150. It was on the April 3rd whilst enjoying himself with friends that Nathanial received a letter from Michael with the good news. The rents had been collected and the bags of gold and silver, along with the rolls of notes, were in the wooden chest hidden behind the secret panel. Michael had also boasted: "The devil himself could never find it."'

Kirkley Hall, Ponteland

'At 8 o'clock the next morning, when Michael went back to Kirkley Hall, he found the door and a glass panel smashed open, the chest ransacked and the money gone. Obviously, the thief had known where to look. When he was informed of the break-in, Nathanial called Detective Lavender from Bow Street, London to find his money. After only a few days at Kirkley Hall, detective Lavender had found most of the money left in shrubbery.

One of the few people who had known about the secret safe was an odd job man; he had worked for four years at Kirkley Hall. James Charlton, known as a very honest and hard-working man, was also very poor and soon became a suspect. James was married with four children and in lots of debt but within days of the robbery, all his debts had been paid in cash. Detective Lavender found witnesses who had seen James in the pub offering to buy friends drinks, waving banknotes around. He was also seen paying six pounds to James Sillick, a leather seller from Newcastle, three pounds to Sarah Kyle and thirteen shillings to Margery Harbottle who ran a grocery shop.

On the May 17th James was arrested by Detective Lavender and taken to Newcastle Keep. He was held in chains until the August assizes. When he went to court, it was to find Michael Aynsley, the person who had been in charge of the stolen money, was also the prosecutor. James Charlton pleaded not guilty and said he had borrowed ten pounds from his brother to pay his debts, which his brother confirmed. James then went on to accuse Michael Aynsley of the crime, bringing in witnesses who told the court Michael had been very nervous after the arrival of Detective Lavender. Also, a servant from Kirkley Hall, Dorothy Hodgson, described how Michael Aynsley had said to her the money would turn up the next day and it had. The defence suggested that Michael Aynsley had stolen the money while Mr Ogle was away; knowing James Charlton had borrowed money so he would get the blame. Giving him the benefit of the doubt, the jury cleared James and he was set free.

While being held at Newcastle Keep, James shared a cell with well-known thief and liar William Taylerson, who told the guards that while he was there Jamie boasted that he got away with the burglary. As William Taylerson was in prison for horse stealing and facing the death penalty, he said he would give evidence against James Charlton if he was reprieved. That was when another prisoner shouted at William 'Would you hang another man just for your liberty?' William answered, 'Yes, liberty is sweet!' On his way to Ponteland, James was again arrested and taken back to court. On the evidence of William Taylerson, the jury this time found James guilty. He was sentenced to life in prison with hard labour.'

We were completely stunned. Our ancestor had been convicted on the word of a condemned horse-thief, who turned King's Evidence and gained his own freedom as a result. The conviction was dodgy even by the questionable legal standards of 1810.

Could Chris be right? Had our James been framed?

I stopped laughing and put down my drink. What had previously just been a fun hobby had now taken a serious turn. We had a miscarriage of justice to explore.

And somewhere in the back of my alcohol-fuddled brain, the seed of another idea began to take root.

'D'you know what?' I blurted out, startled.

'What?'

I savoured the next few words in my mouth like a child who had just tasted ice cream for the first time.

'This would make a cracking story for a book.'

Chris nodded and turned his attention back to the computer, more concerned with the issue of how to gain a posthumous pardon for his four times great-grandfather.

I remained quietly by his side, my mind now racing with possibilities. This genealogy malarkey had now thrown up an amazing opportunity.

The perfect plot for a historical novel had just landed in my lap.

CHAPTER EIGHT
The Quest Begins

Our seven-year-old son, Ross, paused in the middle of his tea with a sausage half way to his mouth. His eyes clouded over with confusion. Chris and I had just spent ten minutes explaining to the children about James Charlton and his dodgy conviction. I sensed immediately we had a problem and suspected that our excitement about the family jailbird had given the children mixed messages. After all, people who go to prison are bad, aren't they?

'Do we have to tell our teachers?' Ross asked, nervously.

'No, sweetheart,' I reassured him. 'It all happened so long ago no one else will mind or care. Your teachers don't need to know – or your friends.'

He sighed with relief and resumed his assault on his bangers and mash.

Apart from this one occasion with our young son, all of our relatives were pleased and excited about our discovery. The two hundred year gap between Jamie Charlton and us has softened the shame of our criminal ancestry and the huge doubt over the validity of his conviction definitely helped everyone to warm to our Regency convict.

It took us five years to research all the details of the robbery and Jamie's conviction.

Fortunately, British criminals are as well-documented as the aristocratic end of the social spectrum; there is plenty of paperwork out there about both the famous and the infamous. During our journey of discovery, we have been bowled over by the kindness of everyone we approached for help. People have gone out of their way to help us gather what information there remains about this two hundred year-old case and the fate of James Charlton.

Our first priority was to track down the court case notes. We found a lady (through the *genuki* online message board) who kept an index of trials at the Northumberland Assize court. She told us James Charlton had been convicted in August 1810.

Our next step was to get hold of copies of the trial documents. Again, we were very lucky. Over the years I have made many online friends with a shared interest in genealogy and Karen Benoy (neé Charlton) and I had become very close.

During those long, fruitless years when we tried to find John and Mary in Elsdon, we had investigated other Charlton families in the village, especially the family of Richard *Charleton* who lived at Todholes farm.

Karen Benoy (neé Charlton) is a direct descendant of Richard Charleton. Apart from our mutual interest in Charlton genealogy, we also both liked the fact that we shared the same name. We met up for coffee on a couple of occasions and even visited the Northumberland records office together.

Karen lived relatively close to The National Archives in London, and she volunteered to try to track down copies of the records in the case of 'The King v. James Charlton'. She successfully located the documents, photocopied them and sent them north through the post. They consisted of thirty-four A3 pages of difficult-to-read witness statements. It took me an entire weekend just to read and decipher the faded, spidery handwriting. But the results were fascinating.

The National Archives, Kew

The clerk recorded the witness statements verbatim, complete with local dialect phrases and the speaker's grammatical mistakes. The only words spoken by Jamie Charlton at his trial were: 'Not guilty' but allegedly, he had held plenty of conversations with the witnesses and so had his wife.

From these, we learnt they both abbreviated their names. 'Jamie Charlton said this'... 'Cilla Charlton told me that...' were common phrases in the transcripts. We pored over every syllable and sentence of these reported dialogues. Jamie and Cilla's voices echoed down to us through the centuries. We have no pictures and it was far too early for photographs, but we do have their words.

We widened our search to the newspapers of the time and discovered that Gateshead Library possessed full copies of the *Newcastle Courant* for the entire period. The trial of James Charlton caused an outcry in Newcastle. The *Courant* was a weekly paper, produced on a Saturday.

James Charlton (and his subsequent appeal) was one of the hottest topics of news and they regularly discussed his case on the front page.

The Ponteland Local History Society also provided me with a useful pamphlet called *The Monthly Chronicle of North-Country Law and Legend (1890)*. It told the story of the case in great detail; the controversy surrounding Jamie and Kirkley Hall still rumbled on eighty years after his conviction. Then the late George Bell, a professional researcher from *Original Indexes*, contacted me. He was researching Northumbrian criminals for a book he was writing and he was interested in the Jamie Charlton story. We shared information and George solved the mystery about what happened to Jamie after he left Northumberland for transportation.

Over the years, I built up a wonderful picture of rural life in the north-east of England in the Regency period. We discovered what agricultural labourers actually *did* to earn a living; how they roamed from farm to farm doing a day's threshing here and a day's ploughing there. We learnt how much the farmers paid them for their labour and what they did in their spare time. They drank brandy (not ale) in the taverns of Northumberland in 1809, gambled on cards and played dice games. Chris and I cringed when we discovered the extent of the debts they ran up during the hardship of a bad winter and the level of credit allowed in the shops they frequented. We now know the price of a cow and a new coat in 1809, and how much reward would be offered if one of their highly-prized sheepdogs went missing.

We learnt about their chapels and the committees they set up to stamp out crime; the pubs where they met and their trips to local markets. We know how much they paid for butter, flour, bed sheets and new boots.

The high level of literacy which abounded in Ponteland in 1809, and across the rest of the north-east also surprised us. All the Charlton brothers could read and write. There were two nearby schools: the Coates School in Ponteland and another in nearby Stamfordham. A large number of the witnesses at the trial signed their own names beneath their statements. The pamphlet written and sold to raise money for Jamie's appeal was for sale in twelve bookshops across Northumberland and County Durham. It is quite a surprise to think that such a remote, sparsely populated area could support twelve bookshops back then. I would be surprised if there are still twelve bookshops in the two counties today. Overall, I have come to the conclusion that the literacy levels in rural England must have been far higher than is generally imagined.

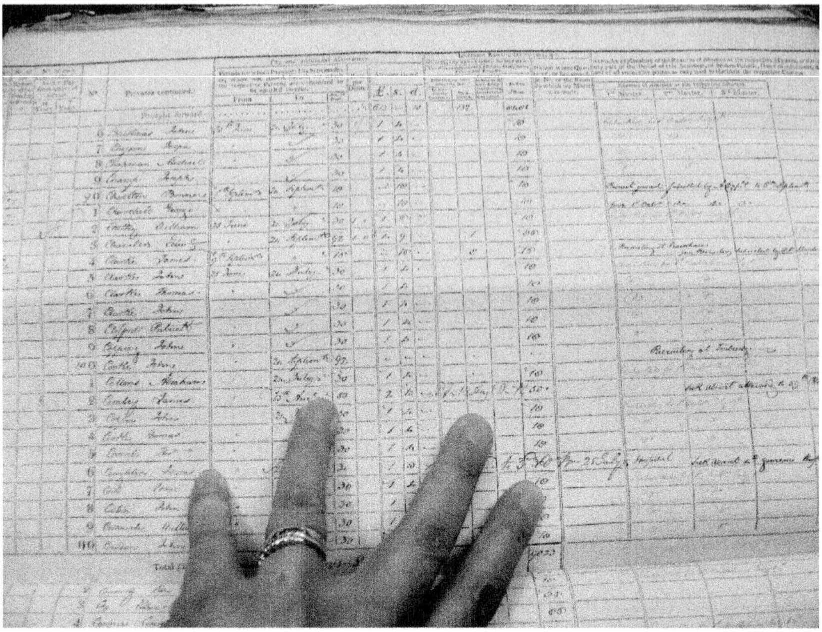

Researching the archives

But our research did not always involve ancient, dusty books and news sheets. Sometimes the research formed part of a fun family day out to Northumberland. Or at least, Chris and I thought it was fun. It turned out that our kids weren't quite so enamoured with our hobby.

Once we all turned up on Open Day at Kirkley Hall, which is now an agricultural college. The staff gave us access to their own information about the burglary in 1809 but strangely enough, would not let us roam freely around the hall.

We could imagine the frantic whispers: 'Quick – lock up the silver! The Charltons are back!'

But we were quite happy to stalk around the edges of Kirkley Hall, in the footsteps of Jamie who probably didn't go inside the building very often. I especially loved the white-washed, rear courtyard of the hall. My imagination pictured it bathed in moonlight, on the night of the burglary.

An incredible, two hundred year-old, Lebanese cedar tree towered above us in the centre of the cobbled yard and I imagined Jamie standing beneath its shade on a hot day back in 1809, perhaps eating the meagre lunch prepared for him by Cilla. I could visualise his scuffed, muddy boots, his hand-made shirt and his frayed coat.

I made a mental note that, somehow, this magnificent tree would feature in my novel.

More Charltons 'case the joint' at Kirkley Hall

On another occasion, we went to see Morpeth gaol, a stark building, which doubled as the town clock tower in 1809. It jutted out of the cobbled market place like a sore thumb.

Morpeth gaol

'There you go, Chris,' I teased. 'This is your great-granddad's last known address in Northumberland. You've finally found the *family pile*.'

'Huh! Some long-lost inheritance, this is!'

'Still got your sights set on Hesleyside Hall, pet?'

'No,' he sighed, sadly. 'But I'd have settled for a small bungalow.'

When the children got older they became more and more reluctant to accompany us on our trips to Northumberland.

'Not *more* graveyards in the rain,' Beth moaned.

'There are some interesting old buildings to see,' I replied.

'For you and Dad, maybe,' she muttered, rebelliously.

'Have you any idea what a sobering experience it was for an eight-year-old to be taken to Morpeth gaol and told your granddad lived there?' Ross complained.

Chris and I looked at each other, surprised.

'I bet none of your friends' parents have taken them on such an unusual trip,' Chris said.

'Exactly.'

'He's a sensitive boy,' I suggested, smiling. 'Perhaps we should just leave them at home with their grandparents?'

So, we did and Chris and I enjoyed exploring the family heritage, alone. Now childless, we had the perfect opportunity to try to track down 'Ma Shotton's' public house, one of the taverns frequently mentioned in the court case notes.

It was a hive of activity in 'Ma Shotton's' on the night after the burglary in 1809. Jamie Charlton threw money around like water and attracted a lot of attention. Allegedly, he offered to buy several people a drink, tried to bet a guinea on a card and bragged about how much gold and silver he had in the pockets of his breeches. We didn't think it would take us long to find such an ancient watering hole in a small town like Ponteland. We were wrong. Ponteland still has at least *three* public houses which are well over two hundred years old.

'You know that we will have to visit them all, don't you?' Chris said. His blue eyes twinkled.

'Give me the car keys,' I replied. I hadn't expected a pub crawl when we drove into Northumberland but this is the trouble with genealogical research; you just never know how it will turn out.

We visited the Diamond, the Blackbird and the Seven Stars. The Diamond and Blackbird retained many of their original features: low beams, large open fire places and unplastered, rough-hewn, interior stone walls. Unfortunately, the Seven Stars had been stripped of everything remotely historic and was now lined with flashy game machines.

True to form, Chris raised a pint of Guinness and toasted his ancestors in all three pubs.

'I've got a tingle down my spine,' he announced ceremoniously in each building. 'Jamie Charlton drank here – I can tell.'

I smiled. The court case notes suggest Chris is probably right; Jamie was no stranger to pubs. We finally discovered that 'Ma Shotton's' was The Seven Stars.

Back in 1809, the landlord of The Seven Stars was called Barny Shotton. In the court case notes, everyone referred to the pub as 'Ma Shotton's', which suggests that she was the dominant personality in the partnership. This gave me a wonderful image of the woman, and when I wrote the brawl scene in the tavern, I described her whacking the miscreants over the head with a broom to get them out of the door.

We later discovered that 'Ma' and Barny are buried in St Mary's church yard, and so is Rob Wilson the toll gate keeper (another minor character in *Catching the Eagle*). My kids may not appreciate a trudge around a muddy graveyard in the drizzle, but for me the physical presence of the historic buildings, the crumbling gravestones and the wonderful rural landscape beneath that big, northern sky, bring these characters and their world to life.

'Ma Shotton's'

Slowly, we gathered up all of the surviving fragments of evidence about the life and trial of James Charlton. Bit by bit, we pieced the story together. And although we still have some gaps in our knowledge, and some of the information is contradictory, we now know more about Jamie and Cilla Charlton than any of our other ancestors.

Chris in St. Mary's churchyard, Ponteland

CHAPTER NINE
Who was Jamie Charlton?

Jamie was born at North Carter Moor Farm in Ponteland and baptised at St. Mary's Church, Ponteland in December 1774. We believe he was the second son of the large Charlton family, who had lived at North Carter Moor Farm for generations, since the 1720s.

North Carter Moor Farm, Ponteland

On November 29th, 1800, Jamie married Priscilla (Cilla) Nimmo of Corbridge. They had five children and John (our ancestor) was the eldest. His siblings, Hannah, Ann, William and Isabella followed at regular two-year intervals. Cilla was eight months pregnant with Isabella when Jamie went on trial for his life. These middle three children were all baptised at Thorneyford Presbyterian Chapel, Kirkley, where the family worshipped at the time of the robbery.

The Family Tree (1774- Present Day)

James (Jamie) Charlton m. Priscilla Nimmo
(b.1774 -)

John	Hannah	Ann (Mary)	William	Isabella
(1802 – 1872)	(1804)	(1806)	(1808)	(1810)

John
Tile maker, Corbridge
m.
Mary Famelton

William m. Margaret Wynn
(1835- 1896)
Stationmaster at Stanhope

John-George m. Phoebe Jacques — 8 other children
(1869 – 1935)
Rail Freight Manager, Middlesbrough

William m. Violet Wilkinson — 9 other children
(1896 – 1953)
Machine Gunner WW1
Plumber, Marske

Arthur Irvin m. Joan McIntyre — 4 other children
(1932 – 2006)
Taxi Proprietor, Redcar

Christopher m. Karen James (school teacher) — Sister
Steelworker, Marske

Two children

From the 1890 pamphlet about the case, we learnt that Jamie was known to be a poor man with a lot of debt but he was also described as 'honest and industrious'. He had been employed for four years as a hind (a retained servant) at Kirkley Hall. But he left this position some years prior to the robbery and eked out an existence as a casual farm labourer. Occasionally he got some work as a cobbler, for which he was trained. At the time of the robbery he lived in the hamlet of Milburn (Milbourne), about two and a half miles from Kirkley Hall, and he worked as a barns man for Robert Gillespy, the farmer at Haindykes (Higham Dykes).

Jamie kept a few cows on the common grazing land around Milburn and grew vegetables on his 'strip'. However, his life was not all about hard work and the chapel. From the court case notes we found at The National Archives in Kew, we discovered Jamie was also a regular visitor to both the Coaching Inn at Newhamm Edge (the modern-day Highlander Inn) and at the Seven Stars public house in Ponteland ('Ma Shotton's').

In 1809 Kirkley Hall was owned by wealthy landowner, Nathanial Ogle, who only visited the hall for a few weeks every summer and who lived for most of the time on his other estate near Southampton.

In Nathanial Ogle's absence, Michael Aynsley, the steward, ran the estate. After receiving Ogle's rent on April 3rd, 1809, Aynsley wrapped the banknotes into parcels, placed them into a canvas bag with the coins, and deposited the whole lot behind a secret panel in an alcove in the estate office. He stacked books and papers in front of it. His arrangement with Nathanial Ogle was to send his employer a letter as soon as the rents were collected and to deposit the money in the bank in Newcastle the next day.

According to the folklore which now surrounds the robbery, Aynsley wrote Nathanial Ogle the letter, which contained these words: 'The rents have been collected; the bags of gold and silver, along with the rolls of notes, are in the wooden chest hidden behind the secret panel. The devil himself would never find it.'

Well, the devil may not have been able to find the rent money but somebody else certainly did. That night, a thief broke into the hall, went straight to the closet which contained the secret panel, scattered the books and papers onto the floor and stole the rent money.

When they discovered the burglary, the servants raised the alarm and sent for Aynsley. Nathanial Ogle was immediately informed and he sent for a principal officer from Bow Street, a Detective named Stephen Lavender, to investigate the crime. Stephen Lavender was a real historical figure. He became the Deputy Chief Constable of Manchester after the formation of the police force by Sir Robert Peel.

Kirkley Hall

We were surprised to discover that there were proper detectives around so early in the nineteenth century. We had previously thought that they didn't materialise until after the police force was established in 1832. I became intrigued by Stephen Lavender and researched his character and career. Apart from assisting with crime fighting on the streets of the capital, the principal officers at Bow Street had a variety of other roles, including espionage for the government's Home Department (a forerunner of the British Home Office). In addition to that, wealthy individuals in the provinces could hire the services of these detectives to help solve difficult crimes, which is what happened in the case of the Kirkley Hall robbery.

During his investigation, Lavender recovered most of the stolen money. It was found in the grounds of Kirkley Hall, close to the public road. Suspicion started to fall on Michael Aynsley who, it turned out, had used that road on the day the money was found.

A servant at the hall, Dorothy Hodgson, recalled that, only the day before, she had held a conversation with Michael Aynsley who said to her: 'Keep a sharp look-out, Dolly; perhaps the money will come back.'

Two other witnesses claimed Aynsley held similar conversations with them, and he said that the greatest part, or all, of the money would come back. Aynsley later justified these comments by claiming it was too large a sum of money for any person to conceal.

The results of Lavender's enquiry were never made public, but shortly afterwards, Ogle dismissed Aynsley from his service; he blamed the steward for the loss of the money. Aynsley was told that 'his employer would certainly look to him for it.' But Aynsley claimed he had received written instructions from Ogle to deposit the money in the closet in the office and that he had nowhere else to secure it, as Nathanial Ogle kept the key to the only 'stronghold'. So unless he took the money home with him that night and risked assault and robbery by the many lawless gangs who roamed the parish of Ponteland, he did not have any choice except to leave the money in the office.

Lavender's enquiry quickly came to the conclusion that whoever broke into the office was thoroughly familiar with the hall and had probably worked there at one time. Suspicion fell on several other people besides Aynsley, including Jamie Charlton. Other suspects mentioned included two brothers called Clifford: one lived at Kirkley, the other in Morpeth. All of them knew about the secret hiding place. However, only the barest hint of possible guilt or complicity was ever brought against the Clifford men.

By coincidence, Jamie suddenly became flush with money about the time of the robbery; he spent a lot and drunkenly flaunted his new-found wealth. Lavender soon came to hear about it and began to collect evidence.

On Easter Tuesday, the day after the robbery, Jamie spent the afternoon in Ma Shotton's public house in Ponteland, where he asked Matthew Mackie, a tailor, to take a glass of brandy with him and to make him up a new coat. Mackie went on to claim that:

'There were other people within the house playing at cards and James Charlton frequently offered to bet a guinea but no person offered to accept the same...I said to him: 'we have wives and families and I cannot think we have much money to spare.'

Charlton replied: 'I have had a hard winter, but I have now plenty of money.' He put his hand into his left-hand breeches pocket and produced some gold. I think that I saw three or four half guineas and several seven shilling pieces. After which he put his hand into the other breeches pocket and produced a great quantity of silver, upwards of twenty shillings...'

Robert Wilson, keeper of the Ponteland turnpike-gate, was also present in the pub on the day after the robbery. He seems to have done a bit of moonlighting as the local debt collector. Several times previously, Wilson had tried to persuade Jamie to pay some, or all, of a large debt which he owed James Sellick of Newcastle for leather, purchased for his shoe making business.

The Toll House, Ponteland (site of the turnpike gate)

That afternoon, however, Jamie said he would treat Wilson and the rest of the company to a crown bowl of punch. He then tapped Wilson on his shoulder and asked him to follow him to the other side of the room. There he told Wilson he intended to settle Sellick's bill, and not by instalments but altogether, which he did a few days later.

Lavender soon discovered that, apart from settling this large bill, Jamie also paid off numerous other debts in the four days which followed the robbery. In fact, he paid off over £15 worth of debt in a week. In addition to this, Jamie spent a lot of money in Newcastle on Saturday April 8th.

Lavender questioned him several times and then, finally, at the insistence of Michael Aynsley, and his two sons, Michael Aynsley Junior and Joseph Bell Aynsley, Lavender arrested Jamie on Tuesday, May 17th, 1809.

However, the detective must have known that there still wasn't enough evidence to convict Jamie of the crime because for three consecutive Saturdays in July, *The Newcastle Courant* ran this advert:

'Two hundred pounds reward

Whereas the office of Kirkley Hall, in the Parish of Ponteland, in the County of Northumberland, was during the night of Monday, the 3rd day of April now last, broken into, and upwards of £1000 taken there out. Whoever therefore will, after this notice, apprehend the offender or offenders, so as he, she, or they may be brought to conviction, shall be paid a Reward of TWO HUNDRED POUNDS upon his, her or their conviction by applying to Nathanial Ogle Esq. of Kirkley.'

The Northumberland assizes were held once a year in August. They moved Jamie to the old Keep, known as Castle Garth Prison, to await trial. Initially, they took Jamie before the county magistrates to discover if there was sufficient evidence to send him to trial at the assizes court.

In his defence, Jamie's younger brother, William, an 'animal husbandman' at North Carter Moor Farm, gave evidence that he had loaned James some money just before Easter. The magistrates found nothing to link Jamie to the crime and threw out the bill against him before it even went to trial. One of the gaolers immediately communicated this news to Jamie through the grille in the door.

It was at this point that a fellow prisoner of Jamie's in Newcastle Keep, a convicted horse-thief called William Taylerson, alleged that in his ignorance, Jamie confused this rejection of a bill with an acquittal from a common jury. Taylerson said Jamie believed he was now safe from prosecution; he believed the double jeopardy law meant he could not be tried twice for the same crime. Confident of his good fortune, Taylerson said Jamie confessed to him that he had burgled Kirkley Hall.

The gaolers released Jamie and he went back to Milburn to celebrate with his family but repercussions followed, both in the law courts and in the streets and taverns of Ponteland. Jamie sued Michael Aynsley and two of his sons for libel and successfully received £5 for each case. In addition to this, the *Courant* mentions 'civil unrest in the streets of Ponteland'. We have not been able to find out the details but the Charltons and the Aynsleys were large families, who all lived on top of each other in a small community and it is not unreasonable to imagine a few tempers flared.

Jamie picked up the threads of his life back in Ponteland, lived another year as a free man and fathered another child, Isabella, with Cilla.

Newcastle Keep

Meanwhile, Taylerson continued to rot in gaol and persist in his claim that Jamie had confessed to him his guilt. Taylerson claimed that Jamie said he was very happy not to have gone before his lordship (the judge), because he feared his own conscience might have condemned him. Taylerson asked why his conscience would have condemned him so long as he was clear. Jamie pointed out that there were more than sixty witnesses against him and added: *"If I had known as much as I know now, I should not have given up a halfpenny of the money."*

"Were you then," said Taylerson, *"guilty of breaking the house?"*

Allegedly, Jamie then confessed to Taylerson he had committed the theft; stated the amount of money he stole and explained how he knew it was there. According to Taylerson, Jamie said he knew Kirkley Hall as well as if he had been born and bred in it. Taylerson claimed Jamie told him that he did the robbery with his wife, Priscilla and a 'neighbour'. Apparently, they tried many doors and windows before they could get in, but eventually Cilla entered by a broken pane in the window and admitted him. Jamie said he found the money easily, but turned over many books and papers before he reached it. He said he was examined four times by the magistrates and would not have been imprisoned the fifth time if his story had agreed with his brother's account about the money which William had allegedly loaned to him. Jamie added, however, that if he and his brother had gone to the bar, their stories would now have agreed as they had taken advice from his attorney.

Jamie, apparently, went on to say that he got up on the Saturday after the robbery between 5am and 6am, went to Kirkley and flung some of the money onto the garden walk. He then proceeded on his journey to Newcastle and saw Aynsley on the road; he climbed over a hedge and hid himself until Aynsley passed.

The Newcastle Courant tells us that a startled Jamie was re-arrested a fortnight before the assizes were due to begin in 1810. His defence lawyer did not have long to assemble his witnesses for the trial, which took place on Wednesday 29th August.

Jamie was tried before Judge Baron Robert Graham. The counsel for the prosecution was led by Mr Topping and a Mr Scarlett, who later earned the nickname 'verdict-getter' in tribute to his ability to manage juries. Mr Topping outlined the facts of the case and then called forward Michael Aynsley, all the witnesses who had claimed Jamie had paid off his debts in the week after the robbery, and he finished with the evidence of William Taylerson.

In his defence, Jamie claimed he was innocent and then left himself in the hands of his counsel. His lawyer called forward several witnesses for the defence who all commented on the curious behaviour of Michael Aynsley at the time of the robbery and re-ignited the suspicion that the wrong man was in the dock. The defence suggested Michael Aynsley stole the money because he knew James Charlton had borrowed money from his brother and he would get the blame.

Other witnesses gave evidence that Jamie was at home on the night of the robbery. Then Robert Gillespy, Jamie's employer, gave evidence. He claimed Jamie always behaved well at his farm and earned a great deal of money from his labour as a barns man. One Joseph Emmerson, whose shop fronted the barn at Haindykes, swore he saw Jamie arrive at work as normal the day after the robbery.

William Charlton, Jamie's brother, now took the stand and claimed that in the weeks before Easter he loaned Jamie twenty pounds. William had previously told several different stories, both about the days he lent Jamie the money and the amount, but he explained the contradictions thus:

'I was never before a magistrate before, and Mr Clennell threatened me so much that I did not know what I was saying or doing, and might then give a different account and swear to it. Mr Fenwick put the questions to me, and said if I did not sign the paper, they would send my brother to prison immediately, and I was so frightened that I signed it.'

Next, a man named William Oliver took the witness stand. He had shared a prison cell with Taylerson in Morpeth Gaol and remembered a conversation with Taylerson about Jamie some two or three weeks after the previous assizes. Taylerson told Oliver that Jamie got discharged without a 'bill' being found, but that he, Taylerson, would gain his own liberty and fetch him in again.

When Oliver said, *"Would you, for the value of your own liberty, hang another man?"*

Taylerson replied: *"Yes. Liberty is sweet."*

The whole trial lasted fourteen hours and finished at 1 o'clock in the morning. The jury retired and after a consultation of only five minutes, brought back the verdict: *"Guilty."*

His Lordship, the judge, remarked that a variety of circumstances favourable to the prisoner had transpired; and he felt that there was still a mystery about the whole case which he could neither unravel nor understand. He suggested an appeal for clemency would be suitable in this case, and then the death sentence was passed in the usual way:

"James Charlton, you are sentenced to be taken hence to the prison in which you were last confined and from there to a place of execution where you will be hanged by the neck until dead."

The case caused great consternation in Newcastle. Many people, including the reporter from the *Courant,* were clearly not satisfied with the verdict.
'The case of James Charlton has excited great surprise... he was found guilty, principally on the evidence of Wm. Taylerson, who received sentence of death at the last assizes for burglary, but who has since obtained his majesty's pardon; and who stated that Charlton confessed to him, when he found that the bill was thrown out in 1809, that he, his wife and another person committed the robbery; and this confession, which according to his evidence, he rendered complete by a most artful set of interrogatories, he asserted was made to him just after he had himself received sentence of death!'

The outcry in Newcastle gained momentum and two weeks later, on 15th September, the newspaper printed this advert:

'James Charlton

At the request of several respectable individuals who feel for the distresses of the unfortunate James Charlton and his family, a subscription has been opened for the purpose of defraying the expense of an Application for his majesty's pardon of the prisoner, and also for the support of his family – a wife eight months advanced in pregnancy, and four helpless young children. Subscriptions will be received by E. Humble & Son, Booksellers, Newcastle.'

William Taylerson claimed Jamie and his wife were thieves. It is obvious from what followed, that many people simply did not believe a word of his testimony. For the next three weeks, the *Courant* listed all the donations made to the subscription. Meanwhile, Mr J. Mitchell of the *Tyne Mercury* wrote an eighteen-penny pamphlet about the trial, entitled *The Trial of James Charlton,* and donated the whole of the profits to the fund. In October, the pamphlet ran to a third edition. They sold it in twelve different booksellers across the north-east: in Newcastle, Durham, Sunderland, Gateshead, North Shields, Morpeth and Alnwick.

We have no idea how much money the fund set up by E. Humble & Son raised, but they printed over a thousand copies of the pamphlet and Jamie got his expensive appeal. In January 1811, the Prince Regent commuted his sentence to transportation to New South Wales:

'His Royal Highness, The Prince Regent, in the name and on the behalf of His Majesty, King George III, was graciously pleased to extend his Royal mercy to the said felon on condition of his being transported to the Coast of New South Wales or somewhere or other of the Islands adjacent for the term of his natural life...'

But there was one final, surprising development to this story before Jamie set off on his journey to the Southern Hemisphere.

He confessed.

On June 8th, 1811 (over two years after the fateful robbery) and witnessed by all three of Northumberland's delighted magistrates, Jamie wrote out a confession in his own hand in the Black Bull in Morpeth. The next Saturday, the startled *Newcastle Courant* published the entire document – complete with his spelling mistakes and lack of punctuation.

In the confession, Jamie claimed that on the night of the robbery he went for a drink at the Coaching Inn at Newhamm Edge (The Highlander) and afterwards found himself mysteriously drawn to Kirkley Hall, where he broke in and stole the money. He said he returned home at 10 o'clock, lied to his wife about where he had been, and never got much benefit from the money he stole, because he hid it in a hole within the chimney breast and it got 'burnt to mush.'

The scene of the confession

Why? Jamie had claimed to be innocent for over two years. Why did he suddenly make this confession? Was he smitten with guilt and a desire to come clean before he disappeared for good? Torture was still used in British prisons in 1810. Did they threaten him with torture?

We firmly believe the authorities forced Jamie to confess so they could reclaim some credibility before the next round of assizes. We also think they threatened to arrest his wife. Our reason for this is contained in his constant assertion that his wife didn't know anything about the robbery, and the very last sentence of his statement, which reads:

'i likewise declare that i had no body along with me when i committed the robery.'

Cilla, his wife and the mother of his five young children, had also been incriminated by Taylerson's damning statement. Jamie was about to be transported to the other side of the world. He had nothing left to gain by confessing but if Cilla was arrested and charged, his children would be left completely defenceless and vulnerable. We believe this confession was the last, desperate act of a man prepared to sacrifice his own reputation to save his family.

And this is the story we intend to tell our descendants.

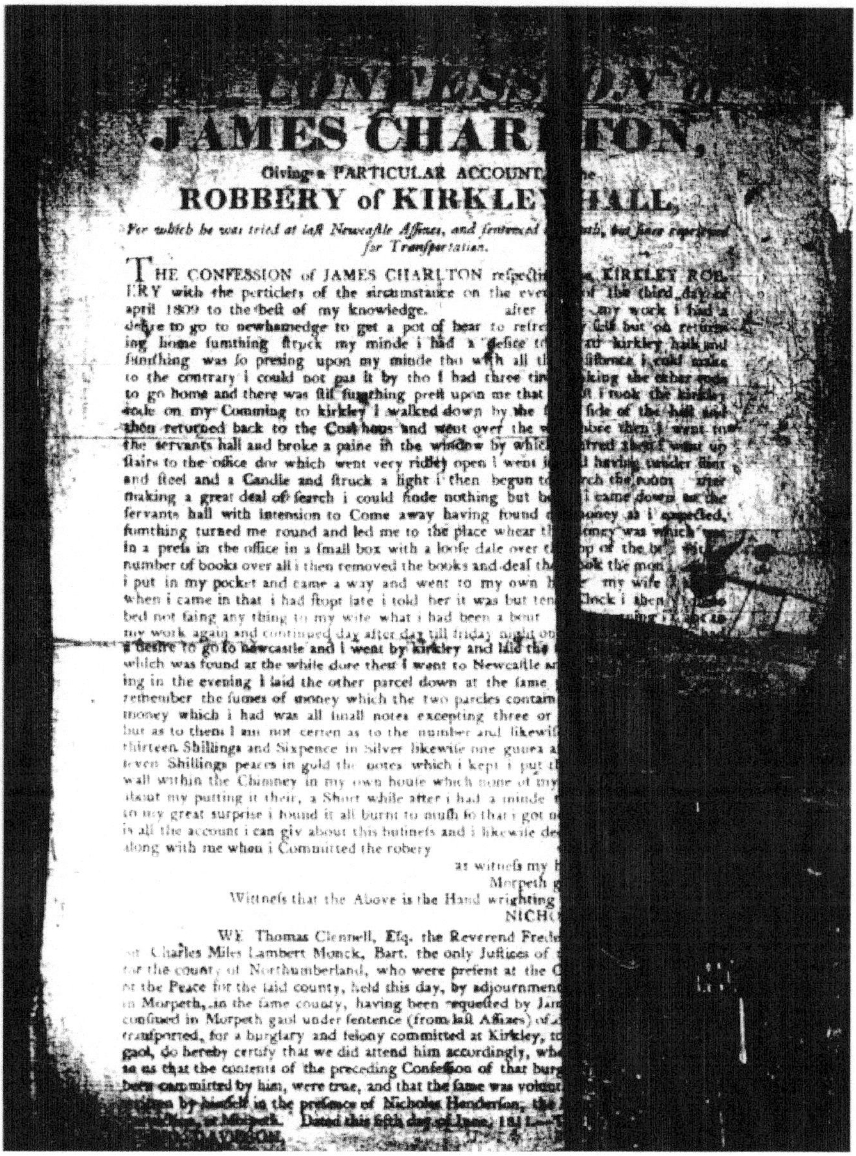

CONFESSION [illegible]

JAMES CHAR[illegible]TON,

Giving a PARTICULAR ACCOUNT [illegible] the

ROBBERY of KIRKLE[illegible] HALL,

For which he was tried at laſt Newcaſtle Aſſizes, and ſentenced [illegible] but ſince reprieved for Tranſportation.

THE CONFESSION of JAMES CHARLTON reſpecti[illegible] KIRKLEY ROBERY with the perticlers of the sircumstance on the eve[illegible] of the third day of april 1809 to the beſt of my knowledge. after [illegible] my work i had a deſire to go to newhamedge to get a pot of bear to refre[illegible] ſelf but on returning home ſumthing ſtruck my minde i had a deſire t[illegible] kirkley hall and ſumthing was ſo preſing upon my minde tho with all th[illegible] diſtance i could make to the contrary i could not pas it by tho i had three tim[illegible]king the other rode to go home and there was ſtil ſumthing preſt upon me that [illegible] i took the kirkley rode on my Comming to kirkley i walked down by the [illegible] ſide of the hall and then returned back to the Coal hous and went over the w[illegible] then i went to the servants hall and broke a paine in the window by which [illegible] then i went up ſtairs to the office dor which went very ridley open i went i[illegible] having tunder ſtuff and ſteel and a Candle and ſtruck a light i then begun t[illegible]rch the room after making a great deal of ſearch i could finde nothing but b[illegible] i came down to the ſervants hall with intension to Come away having found [illegible] money as i expected, ſumthing turned me round and led me to the place whear th[illegible] money was which was in a preſs in the office in a ſmall box with a looſe dale over t[illegible]p of the b[illegible] number of books over all i then removed the books and deal th[illegible]ok the mon[illegible] i put in my pocket and came a way and went to my own h[illegible] my wife [illegible] when i came in that i had ſtopt late i told her it was but ten [illegible]lock i then [illegible] bed not ſaing any thing to my wife what i had been a bout [illegible] my work again and continued day after day till friday night on[illegible] a deſire to go to newcastle and i went by kirkley and laid the [illegible] which was found at the white dore then i went to Newcaſtle a[illegible] ing in the evening i laid the other parcel down at the ſame [illegible] remember the ſumes of money which the two parcles contain[illegible] money which i had was all ſmall notes excepting three or [illegible] but as to them i am not certen as to the number and likewi[illegible] thirteen Shillings and Sixpence in Silver likewiſe one guinea a[illegible] ſeven Shillings peaces in gold the notes which i kept i put th[illegible] wall within the Chimney in my own houſe which none of my [illegible] about my putting it their, a Short while after i had a minde [illegible] to my great ſurpriſe i found it all burnt to muſh ſo that i got n[illegible] is all the account i can giv about this buſineſs and i likewiſe de[illegible] along with me when i Committed the robery

as witneſs my h[illegible]
Morpeth g[illegible]

Wittneſs that the Above is the Hand wrighting [illegible]
NICH[illegible]

WE Thomas Clennell, Eſq. the Reverend Fred[illegible] Sir Charles Miles Lambert Monck, Bart. the only Juſtices of [illegible] for the county of Northumberland, who were preſent at the [illegible] of the Peace for the ſaid county, held this day, by adjournment [illegible] in Morpeth, in the ſame county, having been requeſted by Ja[illegible] confined in Morpeth gaol under ſentence (from laſt Aſſizes) of [illegible] tranſported, for a burglary and felony committed at Kirkley, t[illegible] gaol, do hereby certify that we did attend him accordingly, wh[illegible] to us that the contents of the preceding Confeſſion of that burg[illegible] been committed by him, were true, and that the ſame was volunt[illegible] written by himſelf in the preſence of Nicholas Henderſon, the [illegible] [illegible], at Morpeth. Dated this fifth day of June, 181[illegible]

[illegible] DAVIDSON.

CHAPTER TEN

My Creative Journey into Fiction

I knew from the start that if I didn't sit down at the keyboard and turn this fabulous story into a book then I would never, ever write the best-seller I had always dreamed about. Yet I hesitated and messed around like nobody's business.

I had always been a bit of a scribbler in my younger days and used to write stories in the playground at primary school and force my long-suffering friends to listen to them. When I was eight years old, I put down my latest Enid Blyton and announced to my startled Mum and Aunty Maureen that I intended to be a writer when I grew up. I vividly remember they paused for a moment before they reacted; little girls born into the back streets of Sheffield did not usually grow up to become authors.

Eventually, Aunty Maureen said that perhaps I ought to get a 'proper job' first? I remember I felt a bit crushed at the time, but this was sound advice which I later followed. After Ross was born, I enrolled on a teacher training course (PGCE) at Durham University and within a year I had a job at a secondary school in Stockton.

It is always difficult to find the time to write when you have young children and a full-time day job. I started various novels over the years but never finished any of them. However, I had poetry and some theatre reviews published in local newspapers. For several years I wrote the scripts for *Murder Mystery Weekends* which were performed at the cliff top Raven Hall Hotel, in North Yorkshire.

Raven Hall Hotel, Ravenscar

When I finally found some time to begin the story of Jamie Charlton, I was daunted at the prospect of embarking on an 80,000-word novel. It just seemed too much.

A 'cunning plan' began to form in my head. We never found Baldrick in the branches of my own family tree, but I suspect that he and I are related. I dream up a lot of 'cunning plans', usually with the same disastrous consequences as the TV character.

The ridiculous idea began to take hold that I should write up the story of Jamie Charlton as a radio play for the BBC and I convinced myself I could pull it off. I researched 'How to write a radio play' and I was delighted to discover they were only about 5,000 words long. This encouraged me; I felt I could manage 5,000 words. However, I ignored the bit which says that radio plays have less than half a dozen characters.

I downloaded the format from the BBC website, titled the play 'The Regency Reiver' (after my banter with Chris on the night we discovered his criminal ancestor) and I began to type. Fortunately, dialogue comes easily to me.

I also joined Redcar Writers' Circle and found a fantastic group of people who not only gave me lots of encouragement, but who also read out the parts of the different characters in the script. My brother also volunteered to read the script and gave me valuable feedback. What could possibly go wrong?

Not surprisingly, when I reached 5,000 words, I was only half way through this massive story. Undaunted, I started a sequel and carried on. Naively, I reasoned that BBC Radio Four would have no problem with broadcasting the two plays as a serial.

Yes, the BBC did have a problem with broadcasting the two plays as a serial. In fact, they had a problem with broadcasting these plays, full stop. Plays which contain over thirty characters simply do not work on radio. The rejection slip was kindly worded but it left me in no doubt that 'The Regency Reivers' – volumes one and two – were completely unsuitable for radio.

I wasn't downhearted for long. I was secretly quite pleased that I had actually managed to *finish* the plays. For me, this was quite an achievement in itself. It gave me hope and this exercise left me with 10,000 words of useable dialogue.

Still overawed by the prospect of writing an 80,000-word novel, I developed another madcap scheme. I decided to turn the radio plays into a film script. How hard could this be?

Er, very hard.

I enrolled in an evening class at Teesside University which taught how to write screenplays. The course was great and well taught. The other students (all mature students, like me) were a helpful bunch of people. Unfortunately, I didn't understand a word of it. The structure, terminology and technicalities of screenplays washed over my head like waves over the shingle on Marske beach. I stuck the course out, but by half way through I knew I could never make this work.

However, one great piece of advice I picked up from this course related to William Charlton, Jamie's brother. My fellow students pointed out that whatever form or genre I finally decided to use, I couldn't use Jamie's viewpoint alone. He spends far too much time in Morpeth gaol and page after page of prison life would just get monotonous. I needed someone on the outside looking in; someone closely involved and extremely sympathetic. Jamie needed someone to fight his corner. From this point onwards, the character of William Charlton, Jamie's brother, began to take on a life of his own in my imagination.

After my abortive attempt to write a screenplay, I had no choice left except to stop prevaricating, sit down and write the novel. I began in January 2009, in the quiet lull which follows Christmas and my son's birthday.

On a grid, I laid out all the information we had uncovered. Next, I chose the points in history where my novel was to start and to finish and then began to write chronologically. I hoped to move seamlessly from one event to another. But I had to make some hard decisions at many points during the writing process.

For some of the events, like the court scenes, I had far more information than I needed. Dozens of witnesses gave evidence at Jamie's trial and I needed to make some tough decisions about whom to include and whom to leave out. Many of the statements were very similar but one or two voices and accounts stood out as distinctive and entertaining. The gardener, Ralph Spoors was just pure comedy and Rob Wilson, the Ponteland toll gate keeper who did a bit of moonlighting as the local debt-collector, also fascinated me. I decided to make him an ex-soldier with battle scars and a reputation for brutality: he became the 'hard man' of Ponteland. Conscious all the time that I was writing a novel, rather than a factual account of the trial, it became important to include these entertaining characters.

For other significant events, like Jamie's arrest, I had no information except the date, and I delved deep into my imagination to fill in the gaps. I decided that to create drama, Jamie would be arrested in the most public place I could imagine – the Wednesday Meat Market at nearby Morpeth. At times like these I found Google was my best friend. If I had a query about Regency farming practices or needed to check a legal point to help me and my readers understand the assizes, then I usually turned to the Internet for help.

Morpeth gaol and market place c. 1890

There were also lengthy chunks of time in the chronology of the novel when 'historically' nothing happened – especially when Jamie languished in Morpeth gaol waiting for his trial or the outcome of his appeal, and this is where I switched the viewpoint to the life and thoughts of Jamie's brother, William.

William's story was both a challenge and a joy to write. Historically, Jamie's younger brother remains a mystery. Despite our best efforts and those of the private researcher we eventually employed, we have been unable to find out anything else about William at all. We don't know when or where he was born, what happened to him after the trial or if he ever married. The only reference we have ever found for him related to Jamie's trail. He stood up in court, gave his occupation as 'animal husbandman', his address as 'North Carter Moor Farm' and then gave evidence in support of his brother. He claimed he loaned Jamie twenty pounds just before the robbery.

When it became apparent I needed someone on the outside, to fight for Jamie's cause, who better to use than his loyal brother? Family loyalty became a strong theme in my novel but I knew I needed to make William more complex so I provided him with demons of his own and a conflict of interest. Desperate to break free from the tangled web of family ties which bind him to their small community, he is alarmed to find that he is falling in love with Jamie's wife.

I enjoyed creating William's character. The mystery surrounding him became a blessing not a problem. The lack of historical information about him meant I was able to use my imagination and make him into a romantic hero of my own design. Extra scenes began to appear which fleshed out the story of the Charlton brothers and filled in the gaps between the well-documented historical events.

I have always been really lucky in my friends and family and about this time Zena Breckner and Sam Blain (jokingly known as, *His Excellency the Cultural Attaché for Boosbeck*) volunteered to be readers.

Without the unswerving support and encouragement of Zena and Sam, *Catching the Eagle* would never have been finished. They read it, chapter by chapter, and gave me invaluable feedback and help. They nagged me, criticised me and encouraged me in the way which only good friends can. Very often I forced myself to sit down at the computer and get on with it only because I knew they wanted the next instalment. More often than not, it was their praise which motivated me to run back into the study and write some more.

In the summer of 2010, Chris and I contacted The Ponteland Local History Society. They sent me a copy of the pamphlet about the Kirkley Hall robbery: *The Monthly Chronicle of North-Country Law and Legend (1890).* This was the first time we had heard about the subscription raised for Jamie's appeal and my writing was interrupted while we took several trips back to Gateshead Library to check out the newspaper accounts of the subscription. The chairman of the Ponteland Local History Society also asked me to write a lengthy factual article about Jamie and the robbery for his magazine, *The Pont Island News.* Again, this distracted me from the novel, but it proved a valuable exercise in the long run, as the process of writing this article enabled me to get the chronology of events clear in my mind. With extra chapters needed about the newly discovered subscription, I realised my novel would be even longer than I had originally thought.

After a year of writing, I had about 65,000 words saved on the computer and memory sticks and I naively imagined that I neared the end. At this point Chris took redundancy from the steelworks and became a very happy 'house husband'. I gained more freedom and extra time to write from this change in our circumstances. It also meant we were flush with money for a while. I nicked £150 of his redundancy money and sent off my first three chapters to a recommended Literary Agency in London for a detailed, objective critique.

This was probably the best investment I ever made. A historical novelist read my work and sent me back an encouraging and helpful report, which turned out to be a real eye-opener.

I realised that an English degree, teaching the subject in school and a lifetime love of historical novels does not automatically make anyone – especially me – into an author. Just like creating screenplays, penning fiction is also a craft; it is a skill which has to be practised and honed before it is anywhere near perfect. I was still a long way from perfect.

This literary critic praised my characterisation and dialogue but pointed out that I had major problems with my style, especially with that old chestnut: 'point of view'.

My university education had steeped me in the classics where the authorial point of view abounds. Charles Dickens often jumps into his novels to voice an opinion about the miserable poverty of his characters or the injustice of society. Unfortunately, for modern writers this is not acceptable behaviour. We are supposed to stay out of our own books and let our characters show the nuances of the society they inhabit.

The report made me realise that modern novels don't 'tell', they 'show'. I needed to pick a handful of characters and show the world from their point of view. I needed to show what the characters see, hear, feel, sense and experience and from this my clever readers will make their own minds up about issues like poverty and injustice. I didn't need to point out everything so obviously. Subtlety is the name of the game in good prose.

My critic was right.

Groaning, I settled down and did a massive edit to take 'me' out my novel and to try to address the problem of my style which often head-hopped from the mind and thoughts of one character to another over the space of a few paragraphs.

I was also advised me to dump my 'Prologue' where I introduce the eagle to Ponteland. Apparently, publishers do not like prologues; they are old fashioned and set off alarm bells in the modern publishing world.

This upset me. I loved my eagle and couldn't see how I could introduce the raptor into the parish without the prologue. The whole novel is set beneath the impenetrable gaze of this stray golden eagle, whose fate mirrors that of Jamie's. It is a literary motif which I felt tied the whole book together. In fact, it was about this time I changed the title of the novel from *The Regency Reiver* to *Catching the Eagle.*

I thought long and hard before I decided to ignore this piece of advice. After all, I had paid hard cash for this feedback and I always try to get my money's worth out of every situation (it's the Yorkshire woman in me). But in the end, I did ignore it, although I made an attempt to compromise. I drastically edited the prologue.

As my friends pointed out to me at the time, the report was still ultimately just one person's subjective point of view. This exercise made me realise I needed more objective feedback than just that of family and friends, which is how *Catching the Eagle* ended up on *Authonomy.*

Ponteland

No longer in existence, *Authonomy* was the slush pile of publishers Harper Collins. The idea was that you posted some, or all, of your novel on their website in order to get helpful feedback from the other authors to improve your book. Naturally, you were supposed to reciprocate in kind. There was also a complicated rating system which could send your book up the charts. Those books lucky enough to end up in the top five every month were sent to the Harper Collins editorial desk for a review.

Authonomy was highly addictive and had to approached with a level head and caution. Some authors got caught up in the race for the editor's desk and wasted far too many hours a day on this site. However, the constructive criticism was good, especially if you joined one of the more serious critique groups for your genre, and I made some fabulous friends on this site.

In the autumn of 2010, I announced to the world that I had finished *Catching the Eagle.* The first draft of the manuscript was complete at an unbelievable 120,000 words. I felt an incredible sense of achievement. Yet I knew that for a debut novel, it was now far too long to attract the attention of a publisher, which is quite ironic considering how much I had anguished about my ability to write and complete a full book.

I began another massive edit and this is where my membership of *Authonomy* really helped. Other members on the site often told me to dump my first two chapters.

Originally, I had started the novel with a scene where debt-ridden Jamie asks for more credit and is thrown out of a haberdashery shop. The next ten thousand words then show him in conflict with Michael Aynsley and arguing with Cilla about money. Although some people liked these scenes, many others pointed out that I had promised them a story about a notorious robbery and it took ages to get to the crime.

I realised I had spent far too much time 'setting the scene' and introducing characters and motive, which is a classic new-author mistake. I needed to crack on with the plot. Eventually, I took the plunge, removed Chapters One and Two and edited the novel so it started on the day of the robbery. Fortunately, I was later able to use these chapters as a basis for a short story I wrote for my publisher called *February 1809.* (It is now available in eBook format as a short prequel to *Catching the Eagle.*)

Wary of agents, I decided to first submit the novel to publishing houses who accepted unsolicited manuscripts, but I soon ran out of those and began to work my way alphabetically through the agents in the *Writers' and Artists' Yearbook.* I sent the manuscript out in batches of three and waited six weeks before I repeated the process.

A friend gave me the contact details for Knox Robinson Publishing and they became my thirteenth submission in 2011. Thirteen instantly became my lucky number.

KRP sent me an email which requested the full manuscript for consideration. I had already gone to bed when Chris spotted it in my inbox. This threw him into a terrible dilemma; did he leave it till the morning to tell me – or should he risk a barrage of abuse and wake me up? Snoozing is a favourite hobby of mine and I tend to be rather unpleasant when disturbed.

Eventually, the brave man decided to go with the latter course of action. He came upstairs, shook me roughly on the shoulder and hissed in my ear: 'Don't shout at me. You need to come downstairs and see a message on the computer.'

Half-asleep, I grumbled (but didn't shout) and padded downstairs in my slippers and nightie to read the email. We were ecstatic. It was only a request to see the full manuscript – not an offer of publication – but I had got a toe in the door of a publishing house, albeit a baby toe. Too excited to go back to sleep, we stayed up for hours drinking tea in the kitchen and I did some very dodgy teaching at school the next day and needed matchsticks to hold up my eyelids.

Knox Robinson did not mess about. I had an offer of publication within a week. Not only that, but my new publisher wanted me to write further novels about the Charlton brothers; *The Regency Reivers Series* was born.

I had fulfilled my lifetime ambition to become an author and all those years of research and writing had finally been justified. The long-forgotten story of the injustice meted out to Jamie Charlton would be released into the world, and I would be a published author.
To wake up every day and realise that I have achieved this lifetime ambition, still puts a smile on my face.

Catching the Eagle

CHAPTER ELEVEN

18th Century: A Family at War

Chris and I never intended to stop researching our family history at the story of Jamie and Cilla. Yes, I was busy writing the novel, and yes, it is very hard to go further back in history once you run out of census documents. But we knew there was still more to uncover about the Charlton family.

A small fact in the court case notes, relating to Jamie's brother, William, gave us a clue about where to look next. In his statement to the court, William gave '*North Carter Moor Farm, Ponteland*' as his address. It didn't take us long to uncover an 1806 land tax document online. This revealed that other Charltons were living on the farm at this time. In 1806, a John Charlton held the lease for the farm and paid three pounds, seven shillings and ten pence to Nathanial Ogle in land tax.

We found two more references to John Charlton of North Carter Moor Farm in the newspaper records. The *Newcastle Courant* told us that John Charlton of North Carter Moor Farm sat on a committee determined to bring a Temperance (non-alcoholic) Hotel to Ponteland.

The Temperance Hotel, Ponteland

In addition to this, a month after the burglary at Kirkley Hall, John Charlton is cited in the newspaper with other members of the Ponteland Association for the Prosecution of Felons.

Ponteland Parish Association: For the Prosecution of Felons At our annual meeting held at Ponteland on Monday 3inst. We whose names are hereunder subscribed, have resolved to prosecute with the utmost rigour of the law, all persons who shall be guilty of any Felony, Burglary or any kind of Theft on the Person or Property of any of us the subscribers and that we will amply reward any person who shall be the means of bringing offenders to punishment.

John	*Charlton*	*Carter Moor*
John	*Aynsley*	*Kirkley Thorn*
Aaron	*Charlton*	*Low Callerton*

The irony of these discoveries amused us. If this John Charlton was related to our ancestors, then the suspicion surrounding Jamie, the main suspect in the burglary at Kirkley Hall, must have been a source of deep embarrassment for him. The piety and abstemiousness of this teetotal, law-abiding man would also have been at odds with the habits of Jamie, a drinker and a gambler. I sensed a potential conflict.

We nicknamed him 'Pious John' Charlton and wondered who he was: Jamie's father, perhaps – or another brother? Previous experience had taught us to 'assume nothing.' So we didn't. Ponteland still heaved with many different Charlton families at the turn of the nineteenth century, some related, some not, and we didn't want to jump to any conclusions.

It was the court case notes which gave us our first clue that Jamie had *another* brother, besides the loyal William.

When the horse-thief Taylerson gave his long, rambling statement he claimed that Jamie had mentioned an older brother to him when they shared a cell in Morpeth gaol. Although everything Taylerson said must be taken with a pinch of salt, we paid particular attention to this part of his statement:

'...he (Jamie) said he stole the money to pay off some small debts and buy a cow but he had not borrowed twenty pounds off this brother and he further said if it had been his elder brother instead of his younger they could not have committed him.'

To us, this suggested that the local community respected Jamie's elder brother and his word would not have been doubted.

Next, we checked out the Ponteland baptism records and discovered that a John and Jane Charlton at North Carter Moor Farm baptised six children between the years of 1795 – 1805. This is roughly about the same time Jamie and Cilla's children were born, which implies John Charlton and our Jamie were about the same age.

Everything began to fit together like a jigsaw puzzle. These baptisms, Taylerson's statement and the articles we had uncovered in the newspapers, all suggested there was a *third* brother, who ran North Carter Moor Farm where William worked. 'Pious John' Charlton, the farmer of North Carter Moor, began to form in my imagination and feature in my novel. I portrayed him as a man whose moral values often conflicted with those of his brothers, Jamie and William.

North Carter Moor Farm

But we needed help to confirm our suspicions. Completely absorbed in my novel-writing, I had no time for further research. In addition to this, to track down ancestors in the late eighteenth and early nineteenth centuries, I would have had to spend hours on the dreaded microfilm readers. The Northumberland records are also very difficult to decipher for this period. The job needed someone with more time, patience and stamina than us; so we banded together with other family members and paid for a private researcher.

He did an excellent job and quickly confirmed that our ancestors *were* related to the Charltons of North Carter Moor Farm.

In fact, he discovered that Jamie and his brothers were the *third* generation of Charltons to live at the farm. Jamie's father was also called John and he was descended from *another* James Charlton (1700-1770) who moved to the farm with his first wife, Elizabeth Gofton, back in the 1720s. Their first son, Henry, was born there in 1729.

Elizabeth Gofton m. James Charlton m. Isabel Anderson
(1705-1736) (1700-1770) (1706- 1772)
Farmer of North Carter Moor

Mary (1727) Henry (1729) Aaron (1732) Isabel (1735) James 1739) Edward (1740) William (1741) Ann (1743) Margaret (1749)

John (1746)

John (1769) James ('Jamie') (1774) William (born ?) Henry (1776)
m.
Priscilla Nimmo

The Charltons of North Carter Moor

The daughter of the wealthy Gofton family of Eland Hall, Elizabeth Gofton was a bit of posh totty. She bore James Charlton (senior) four children but died soon after the birth of their second daughter and is buried in the Gofton family vault in St. Mary's Church, Ponteland.

On November 26th, 1738, James (senior) married again to Isabel Anderson. It is this second wife, Isabel, from whom we are descended, not the highly-esteemed and gentrified Elizabeth Gofton.

On our next visit to Ponteland, Chris and I went to the churchyard and tried to find the graves of our family members; there weren't any left. A bit dispirited, we wandered into the cold, empty and echoing church and found the ornate Gofton vault, half hidden in the gloom behind the organ.

'So Elizabeth Charlton neé Gofton is not related to us?'

'No love, she was our ancestor's first wife – we are descended from his second wife's children.'

'I guess we're just not destined to find links with the landed gentry,' Chris observed, sadly.

'The local criminal fraternity, maybe,' I replied with a wink. 'The landed gentry: no.'

He sighed and I could see his hopes of discovering that 'family pile' fading from his eyes. I linked my arm in his.

'Never mind. You never know – my novel and Jamie Charlton might bring us fame and fortune.'

He smiled, sceptically: 'Yes, maybe. But don't give up the day job just yet, Karen.'

Isabel Anderson, the second wife of James (senior) bore him six children. Their youngest son, John (born in 1746) was our ancestor. Despite his five older brothers, John (1746) eventually became the sole tenant of the farm. This surprised us; in their world, primogeniture dominated and the younger sons usually ended up as agricultural labourers, like Jamie.

The family's eldest son, Henry, emigrated to Nova Scotia in the 1760s and spawned a huge tribe of his own who went on to populate most of Canada. So, he was well out of the picture when it became time to hand over the lease of the farm. The two eldest daughters, Mary and Isabel, eventually left home to get married. However, the rambling and isolated farmhouse must have been very overcrowded at times.

By the time of the death of James Charlton (senior) in 1770, there was clearly a lot of conflict and dissention amongst the members of the family. We know this because our researcher discovered a will made by James (senior) just before the farmer died. In the 1770s, very few people made a will. James (senior) was obviously worried about what would happen to his estate, his wife and his sick son, Edward (1740) after his death. He instructed his lawyer to write down his wishes in great detail and threatened his heirs with expulsion from the farm if they didn't behave.

James Charlton's Will 1770

'...after all are valued and everyone knows their just part, I will that the farm be carried on in the same manner by my wife and Aaron and John and all my family to continue on my farm as they are so long as they please, and James I disallow to have any right at all to the farm during my

lease and for the good behaviour of Aaron or John or any one of them while they continue together I appoint my brother Henry Charlton and Robert Nicolson to look to take to authorize them to see and look that they behave themselves as they ought towards my wife and son Edward, and that they carry on their business in a right and orderly manner and in case of any misdemeanour I desire the aforesaid Henry Charlton and Robert Nicolson to rebuke and admonish and pray them to do well...if either Aaron or John behave not well towards my wife, my son Edward or any of my family then I appoint constitute authorize and allow the aforesaid Henry Charlton and Robert Nicolson to turn either Aaron or John off the farm in case of bad behaviour neglect of business or the like...'

North Carter Moor Farm

This document paints a startling picture of a family at war. I can imagine the claustrophobic atmosphere at the farm and the tension between Aaron, the older son, and his step-mother. It is also clear that nobody liked Edward, the sickly brother (who died two years later) and the will suggests his siblings were cruel to him.

In another dramatic phrase in the will, son James (1739) was completely disowned. We have no idea what this lad did to deserve disinheriting and can only assume it was pretty horrendous by the standards of 1770. Which means it must have been, well, pretty horrendous. I see a lot of similarities between North Carter Moor in the eighteenth century and the story of Jacob and his twelve feuding sons in the Bible. Personally, I suspect that James (1739) angered his father when he tried to sell sickly brother Edward into slavery with a passing camel-train of Scots.

'I get the impression that James is not a lucky name for the Charltons,' I said to Chris. 'First of all we have Jamie 'the wronged man in Morpeth gaol' who gets himself transported and then another generation back, we discover his uncle James is disinherited by his father!'

'Yes,' Chris murmured. He shot me an accusing glance. 'And you insisted we give *our* son 'James' as a middle name?'

Ooops. Hindsight is a wonderful thing.

In addition to the unexplained mystery of the disinherited James (1739) another son, William (1741), is barely mentioned in the will; James (senior) leaves him a meagre half a crown compared to the ten pounds each he leaves to Aaron and John.

Favouritism was clearly rife in this household. Just like Jacob in the Bible, James (senior) had his favourite sons; Edward, Aaron and John were at the top of the pile, William languished in the indifferent middle and bad-boy James (1739) was way, way down at the bottom. In the end, James (senior) tore the multi-coloured coat of many colours in two and he left the lease and joint control of North Carter Moor to Aaron and our ancestor, John. They must have been the Geordie equivalent of Joseph and Benjamin. However, even this decision was conditional on their good behaviour.

This all seems a far cry away from the close bond shared by William and Jamie forty years later, when William risked a charge of perjury to stand as a witness for his brother. In fact, in some ways, Jamie and William come across as a pair of angels compared to their feuding father, aunts and uncles. It is also a far cry away from the much-lauded tribe loyalty of the Charlton Border Reivers who roamed this landscape a few centuries before and thundered into Hexham to break Topping Charlton out of gaol.

James Charlton (senior) died two days after he made this will and they buried him in Ponteland Church yard. At the very least, his Last Will and Testament reveals his controlling nature; at its worst, it suggests a fractious and dysfunctional family life existed at North Carter Moor.

James's sickly son, Edward, and his wife, Isabel, died two years later and are buried with him. The actual grave has disappeared but a

Monument Inscription service has recorded the writing on the gravestone for prosperity. The family tombstone read:

Here lies the body of James Charlton of North Carter Moor who after a pious humane and respected life died June 12th 1770 aged 70 years also Isabel his wife no less esteemed than her husband died March 19th 1772 aged 66 years also Edward their son died August 1772 aged 33 years.

We have no idea if Uncle Henry and Robert Forster were ever called upon to rebuke or admonish John (1746) and Aaron (1723) over how they ran the farm and treated the rest of the family, but the whole episode is probably worthy subject matter for another novel.

According to the land tax documents, the two brothers shared the lease of the farm for several years before John Charlton (1746) became the only farmer at North Carter Moor. We believe Aaron moved onto a different farm at Low Callerton. Either that or John murdered him, chopped up his body and fed it to the pigs.

John was the father of the brothers in my novel and at the moment we know very little about him or his wife, Jamie's mother. However, we later discovered that John (1746) was still alive at the time of the Kirkley Hall robbery and this gave me a dilemma.

Should I include both the father *and* Jamie's eldest brother, 'Pious John', as characters in the book? If so, how should I deal with the problem that they were both 'Johns?' In the end, I decided to kill off Jamie's father early, and leave 'Pious John' in charge of the farm. There are just too many 'John Charltons' in our family tree for even the most dedicated reader to follow the plot.

Returning to the 'scene of the crime'

As a final note to a chapter dedicated to our ancestors at North Carter Moor, I feel I must mention our latest adventure at the farm.

In the summer of 2011, Chris and I went back to Ponteland armed with the camera. Determined to photograph as many places we could which were linked to our genealogy and the places mentioned in *Catching the Eagle,* North Carter Moor Farm was at the top of our hit list.

Chris, yet again, announced his intention to drive into the farmyard at North Carter Moor and introduce ourselves. I grimaced and steeled myself for another encounter with a startled pair of Northumbrian farmers.

As Robbie Burns would say: *'The best laid schemes o' Mice an' Men, Gang aft agley... '*

The farm is not easy to find and it is guarded by a herd of curious young cows, who soon gathered behind the barred metal gate which blocked the road. They stared quietly at us from beneath the long-fringed eyelashes of their large, brown eyes.

'Nip out and open the gate,' Chris said.

I eyed the animals dubiously; I wasn't taken in by their placid appearance. I had endured my first terrifying experience of cows when I was only five years old and my own children were a similar age when I dragged them at great speed up a steep hill to escape from a playful bullock in Wensleydale. Ever since then, Chris has carried a large stick nicknamed the 'cow (or bull) whacker' on our family walks in the countryside. Unfortunately, he doesn't keep one in the car. Apart from my handbag, I had nothing to hand which I could use as a 'cow whacker'. I knew I would never be able to wield a handbag with the same legendary ferociousness as the ex-prime minister, Margaret Thatcher, so I felt rather vulnerable.

Meanwhile, Chris, the perfect gentleman, remained firmly in the driver's seat.

Slithering in the mud (and God knows what else) in my inappropriate town shoes, I nervously approached the gate, unlocked it and pushed. At first, the cows scampered away as the gate screeched and the engine revved. Chris drove through without incident and pulled over to wait for me to close the gate and climb back in.

As soon as I turned my back, the cows began to slowly and silently creep up behind me. I could feel them sidling closer. The hairs on the back of my neck shot up like a cat's. Chris wasn't the only one to get tingles in his spine during that trip.

I slammed the farm gate shut and sprinted squealing back into the car quicker than an Olympic 100-metre athlete, which is quite impressive considering the height of my heels.

We pulled into the farmyard at North Carter Moor, armed with a copy of the family tree to prove that we were who we said we were and hadn't just turned up to case the joint (well, you never can tell with us Charltons, can you?). I knocked on the door to ask if we could take a few photographs. Sadly, no one was at home.

We waited for a while and then decided to be cheeky, stalk around the edges of the farm and take a few photographs anyway. Conscious that somebody, somewhere, may have seen us and would report our suspicious behaviour back to the owners, I scribbled out an explanatory note and shoved it through the letterbox.

At this point, I reasoned that the situation could go one of two ways: either the current owners of North Carter Moor Farm would choose to log onto my website and discover some more about the history of their home; or, they would instruct their solicitor to sue us for trespass, breach of privacy and disturbing the peace of their cows.

North Carter Moor Farm

. But we heard nothing and I completely forgot about our little escapade until seven months later.

In March 2012, 'The Friends of Kirkley Hall' invited me back to 'the scene of the crime' to give a talk about *Catching the Eagle.* Despite joking that they would frisk us for stolen goods as we left the premises, the modern custodians of Kirkley Hall opened their door to the descendants of Jamie Charlton and gave us a warm welcome. I had a fabulous night and afterwards signed copies of the novel for the guests.

Imagine my shock when two of the guests came over and introduced themselves as the current owners of North Carter Moor Farm. This was a scary moment. Startled, my first thought was that they had come to serve me that outstanding writ for trespass.

Fortunately, they just wanted me to sign their copy of the novel. It seemed they bought a copy of the book for Christmas, only days after it was published.

I shouldn't have been surprised really. Not by the warmth of our welcome at Kirkley Hall or by the bemused support given to my novel by the current owners of North Carter Moor Farm. Every Northumbrian we have ever met has been pleasant, cheerful, laid-back and more than willing to go out of their way to help us. When you combine this with their fabulous accent and a great sense of humour, I think it is easy to see why the friendliness of these people is legendary. Yes, history has proved that a few of them can be rogues but England's most northerly county is still our favourite British holiday destination – and the local people are part of the reason for this.

Signing copies of the novel at Kirkley Hall.

CHAPTER TWELVE
'Heiress'

When we found James (senior's) will of 1770, it inspired me to create the Carnaby family of Linn Hagh for my second novel which I originally called, *The Missing Heiress.*

In the spring of 2011, while I submitted *Catching the Eagle* to publishers and agents, the first seeds of a plot for another book, a whodunit, began to germinate in my head, based on a dysfunctional family living in a remote location. I've always enjoyed a good crime, a fact which is borne out by all those *Murder Mystery Weekends* I wrote many years ago for Raven Hall Hotel. Before I knew it, I had a Regency mystery to solve and as far as I was concerned there were only two policemen in England who could crack this case.

When I wrote *Catching the Eagle,* I thoroughly enjoyed creating the characters of Detective Stephen Lavender and the comical, good-natured Constable Woods, and I didn't want to let them go. Ultimately, Lavender was the man who placed our ancestor, Jamie, in the dock but we don't hold this against him. The strong personality of the intelligent detective became one of my favourite characters and the dialogue and rapport which developed with his fictional assistant was fun to write. I felt I had created a winning duo of Regency crime-fighters.

I decided my next novel would be spin-off from my first and feature the two policemen. As the plot unfolded inside my head, I determined that the unusual Last Will and Testament of James Charlton (senior) would also appear somewhere in this new novel, and it does. I lifted the contents of his Last Will and Testament and recreated them, virtually word for word, into the will of Baxter Carnaby.

Set in Northumberland in 1809, the first case in this new series takes Lavender and Woods back to Northumberland to investigate the mysterious disappearance of a beautiful heiress. Convinced, at first, this is just a simple case of a young woman who has eloped with a lover, Lavender and Woods are alarmed to discover the sinister world of madness, violence and secrets which lurks behind the heavy, oak door of the ancient Pele Tower at Linn Hagh.

I enjoyed writing *Heiress*. It slid off my keyboard like silk, and I finished all 85,000 words in ten months. Unlike *Catching the Eagle,* which is based on a true story, *Heiress* is pure fiction. I never felt constrained by historical fact and it was an unfettered pleasure to write.

For a woman who once struggled to write a 5,000-word radio play I had now become a prolific writer – and this time I decided to use only three points of view. My writing critic from the Literacy Agency would be proud of me.

I particularly enjoyed creating the female characters. *Catching the Eagle* is dominated by men because the historical records decreed it so; they dominated the crime, the investigation and the court case. In *Heiress,* I created a diverse range of women, from the delightful young maid, Anna, to the mysterious gypsy girl, Laurel Faa Geddes and the intelligent Katherine Armstrong. I loved breathing life into these women and hope I gave them a significant voice in this book.

Heiress was first published by Knox Robinson Publishing on December 6th, 2012, under its old title, *The Missing Heiress.*

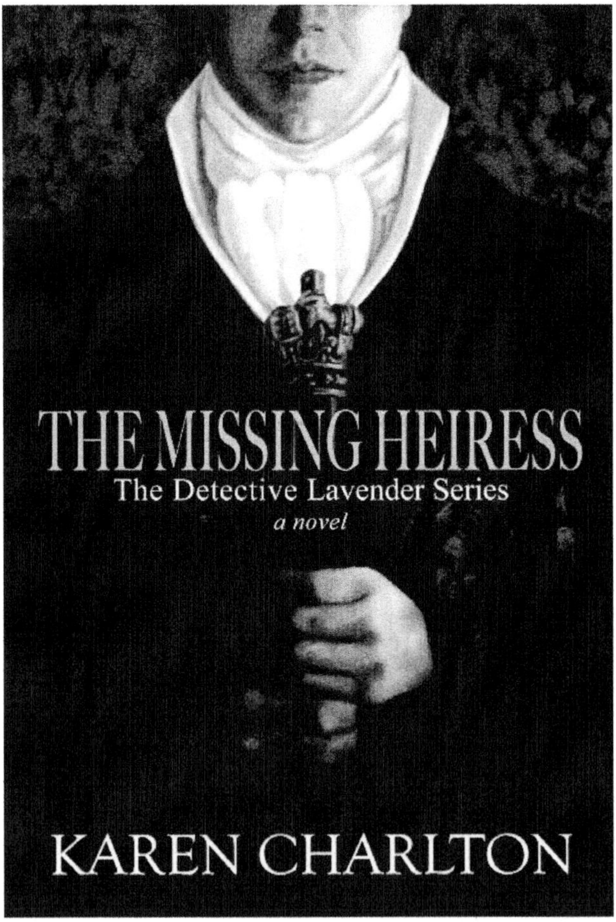

But by the time *Heiress* was published, my relationship with Knox Robinson had already soured. Like many small publishers, they did little to market the novel, relying instead on the energy and enthusiasm of the authors to sell the book. The books were overpriced and hard to sell. Recently I wrote a tongue-in-cheek blog article based on my own experiences and those of my author friends. It sums up our feelings about small publishers.

1. You probably won't be paid an advance and won't see a penny in royalties until six months after the book is published.
2. In the meantime, you will be expected to do an awful lot of marketing to promote the book and this will cost money – a surprising amount of money. You will buy in lots of stock, organise expensive book launches which no one attends and travel up and down the country to poorly-attended events where no-one buys your book.
3. You will annoy and pester your teenage children into designing web pages for you. And beg them to teach you about Facebook and Twitter.
4. You will rapidly lose friends – especially on Facebook and Twitter – as you harass everyone you know into buying your book.

5. Those family and friends who do read your book will make the most bizarre assumptions about upon whom the characters are based.
6. You will soon realise you're spending more time marketing your first novel than you are writing the second one.
7. Despite having no publicist or marketing budget, you harbour a secret hope that somehow your novel will make it onto the bestseller list and be signed up for a film deal. You will dream of retiring from the day job, moving to the Mediterranean and spending the rest of your life sipping cocktails beside the pool, while tapping out another best-seller on the laptop.
8. Everyone else in the world will assume you're coining in the cash, while you may have an uneasy suspicion that this is just turning out to be a VERY expensive hobby.
9. When your first royalty cheque arrives, you will be devastated, convinced there should be another zero at the end of that figure. At this point, your long-suffering partner will lose patience with you and refuse to support you or your writing any more. If you're really unlucky, your publisher will fold and disappear off into the ether, still owing you money.
10. Despite the fact that your spouse has filed for divorce and the bailiffs are on the doorstep, no-one will ever have any sympathy for you...because you're a writer 'living the dream'.

Well, Chris didn't file for divorce – but he did share my disappointment. The disillusionment I felt overwhelmed me. Completely demotivated, I stopped writing; there was nothing to write for any more.

In the summer of 2013, Knox Robinson Publishing asked all their authors to rip up their current contracts and sign another one. At this point I chose to jump ship. As you will see in the next chapter this was probably the best career decision I have ever made in my entire life.

CHAPTER THIRTEEN
The Final Chapter

"The best laid schemes o' Mice an' Men,
Gang aft agley,
An' lea'e us nought but grief an' pain,
For promis'd joy!"
- Robbie Burns (1785)

In the first edition of this book, I wrote hopefully about my plans to continue our family history research and write a second novel about that rogue, Jamie Charlton. We had tantalising leads about what happened to him after he left Ponteland for transportation to Australia.

Chris and I also hoped to continue with the genealogical research and try to take the family tree back further than 1700. We had traced our Charlton ancestors through eight generations and three centuries, to the birth of James Charlton (senior) in 1700, which was a tremendous achievement in itself. For the five generations above him, Chris was the eldest surviving son of the eldest surviving son, with his claim to the 'family pile' undisputed. Unfortunately, we fell at the last hurdle. Now some Canadian Charlton, a descendant of Henry (1729) will one day be able to lay claim to the ancestral Charlton pile.

Chris desperately wanted to find a link with the Border Reivers but our research was still a century and more away from them and 'Topping Charlton'. So many questions still remain unanswered.

Where did our last known ancestor, James Charlton (senior) come from? How did he attract such a high status first wife like Elizabeth Gofton from Eland Hall? Have we stopped at the point in history when it gets interesting? Maybe James (senior) was the younger son of a family of landed gentry, himself?

Then there are the larger questions about those momentous moments in British history which would have affected even the most isolated lives in rural England. On whose side were the Carter Moor Charltons during the Jacobite rebellion? And what about the earlier English civil war? How did this affect them?

TEN GENERATIONS OF CHARLTONS

Elizabeth Gofton m. **James Charlton (Senior)** m. **Isabel Anderson**

Farmer at North Carter Moor

(1705-1736) **(1700-1770)** **(1706- 1772)**

Four children Five siblings **John (1746)**

'Pious' John (1769) **James ('Jamie') (1774) m. Priscilla Nimmo** William (born ?) Henry (1776)

John
(1802 – 1872)
Tile maker, Corbridge
m.
Mary Famelton

Hannah (1804) Ann (Mary) (1806) William (1808) Isabella (1810)

William m. Margaret Wynn
(1835- 1896)
Stationmaster at Stanhope

John-George m. Phoebe Jacques
(1869 – 1935)
Rail Freight Manager, Middlesbrough

8 siblings

William m. Violet Wilkinson
(1896 – 1953)
Machine Gunner WW1
Plumber, Marske

9 siblings

Arthur Irvin m. Joan McIntyre
(1932 – 2006)
Taxi Proprietor, Redcar

4 siblings

Christopher John m. Karen James (School teacher)
Steelworker, Marske

Sister

Elizabeth Amy Charlton **Ross James Charlton**

Sadly, these questions will remain unanswered in my lifetime. I will never pick up the threads of our genealogical research again. There is no easy way to explain what happened next.

In January 2012, Chris was diagnosed with terminal pancreatic cancer.

This diagnosis came out of the blue after he went to the surgery complaining about indigestion. It was stark and brutal. We were devastated. At the time, our distraught children, Beth and Ross, were aged seventeen and fifteen.

Yet despite our misery, Chris forced to us to keep hoping and somehow this helped us to get up every day and carry on with our lives.

'We're going to keep on hoping for a miracle right until the last day,' he said. His courage and strength were amazing.

He put himself through four rounds of chemotherapy. The first two gave spectacular results and briefly we thought that we might have our miracle. Then the tumour mutated and spread. For eighteen months after his diagnosis, my loving, uncomplaining and tenacious husband clung onto his life, determined to stay with me and his children for as long as he possibly could.

Chris died on June 13th, 2013.

The weather was beautiful that summer. But for me, those months were a blur. My life had been ripped apart. I'd lost my lover, my best friend, my companion and my partner in crime. I also felt overwhelmed with the responsibility of being a single parent to two grieving children and I was terrified I wouldn't cope on my own. My family and friends couldn't have been kinder and more supportive but it was hell trying to learn to live without him. I spent every day, that summer, stumbling around the garden, trying to dig and weed through a veil of tears. It sounds banal but it helped. I felt close to Chris in the garden and found comfort in simple tasks and the gentle rays of the sun.

I took a voluntary redundancy from my teaching job. When the kids went back to their respective educational establishments in September, they had a stay-at-home Mum for the first time in their lives. I was there if they needed my help. We were still working through our grief and were more forgetful and absent-minded than normal. The slightest little problem quickly escalated into a crisis. I needed to be at home with my kids.

I had a vague plan that after a year, when I had run out of money, I would return to supply teaching. In the meantime, I started to pick up the pieces of my literary career. The publishing rights to my two novels reverted to me in January 2014 and I was suddenly motivated again. I renamed *Heiress*. I organised proper editing and proofreading for the books and had new covers designed. For the first time in years I thought about writing a new novel. Another Detective Lavender story began to form in my mind.

I always knew that *The Heiress of Linn Hagh* was my most commercial book. Crime fiction, even historical crime fiction, is one of the most popular genres on the planet. So, I decided to self-publish this novel first. It came out in February 2014. For the first two months, I made a handful of sales.

In April, the eBook sales in the USA suddenly took off. This happened while I was away on holiday in Turkey with the children and I'm still not 100% sure what the catalyst was which kick-started my sales. However, I think it may be a favourable review I received from Cathy Cole, one of Amazon's Vine Reviewers. Cathy was kind lady, who liked my novel. I now realise that she must have a large group of followers in the States. When I came back from Turkey, Cathy's review had been posted and *Heiress* was now selling about ten eBooks a day in America on Amazon.com.

And most importantly, it gained a low rank in the Amazon sub-category: Historical Mysteries. These rankings are important because browsing readers can suddenly see your book. Being visible, and staying visible, in a popular Amazon sub-category is the key to success for self-published authors.

I put the price down to $0.99 in order to make it more attractive and to try to keep the momentum going. Desperate to keep the eBook visible in those rankings, I entered *Heiress* into a promotion and sold another 200 copies in the States. To my delight, dozens of new and positive reviews also began to appear. It seemed that the Americans couldn't get enough of my Regency mystery set in rural Northumberland.

I was over the moon. After so much frustration and such a disappointing start with my previous publisher, *Heiress* was finally being read – and enjoyed. All those years of hard work had paid off. My precious novel had found an audience at last.

On one hot, giddy day in August, I sold an incredible 130 eBooks. Or rather, on one hot, giddy NIGHT I sold 130 eBooks. Because of the time difference between the UK and the US, most of my sales happened at night. I'd go to bed and when I checked my sales first thing in the morning, I was often hundreds of dollars richer. It's definitely the best way for a woman to earn money while lying on her back. I can highly recommend it.

Conscious that my reviewers wanted more stories, I turned my attention to my other novel. I self-published *Catching the Eagle* in July 2014.

I also published a short story I had lying around about Detective Lavender called *The Mystery of the Skelton Diamonds* and I hastily wrote another one: *The Piccadilly Pickpocket.* Both the short stories and *Catching the Eagle* began to sell well in the States, in the wake of the success of *Heiress.*

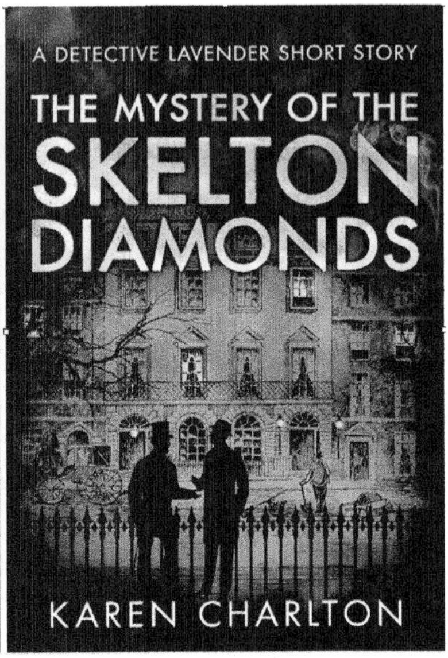

By October I had sold 13,000 eBooks; 99.9% of them in the US. Paperback sales had also taken off. At one point, my royalty payments were higher than the salary I received when I taught at a British secondary school. There would be no more talk of returning to teaching. Motivated and happy, I sat down and began to write a second Detective Lavender novel: *The Sans Pareil Mystery.*

Then, in October, I had the most amazing experience.

I was head-hunted by Emilie Marneur, the Senior Acquisitions Editor from Thomas & Mercer, an imprint of Amazon Publishing. She wanted my Detective Lavender Series to publish under their Thomas & Mercer crime fiction imprint. She had read *The Heiress of Linn Hagh* and loved it. She wanted to know if there was any chance we could work together on the series.

After some discussion, she offered me a jaw-dropping deal in order to take over *Heiress* and publish *The Sans Pareil Mystery.* I know that it was jaw-dropping because my mouth didn't formulate words properly when I phoned my sister later.

I live a quiet life in a sleepy English fishing village where nothing ever happens. As a rule, senior editors from major publishing companies don't just materialise unbidden out of the autumn mist and offer Marske residents amazing publishing deals.

I asked Emilie how she had heard about me. Why had she picked out me from the hundreds of thousands of self-published authors on Amazon? She just laughed, kept her secrets and said she had 'special antennae'.

However, I have no doubt that an Amazon computer must have highlighted the fact that a middle-aged ex-teacher in the remote north of England was selling shedloads of her historical whodunit on amazon.com. This set off a chain reaction in Amazon HQ which resulted in Emilie's email and the offer from Amazon Publishing.

The Heiress of Linn Hagh had her third makeover in three years and was published by Thomas and Mercer on June 9th 2015. Three months later, they published the second novel in the series: *The Sans Pareil Mystery*. This was followed by *The Sculthorpe Murde*r in 2016.

Signing with Thomas & Mercer has been the best move I've ever made in my life. The series has now sold a quarter of a million books and the fifth book, *Death of a Lothario* will be published in March 2019.

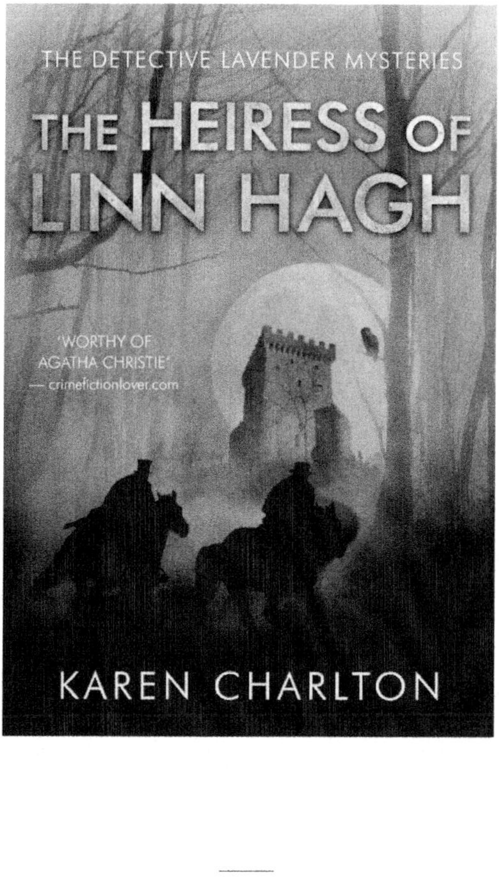

Thomas & Mercer have helped me to reach hundreds of thousands of new readers I couldn't reach myself.

And after all, this is why writers have that compulsion to write, isn't it? To tell our stories to as many other people as possible. I feel incredibly lucky that I have been able to realise my dream and I hope that my experience helps somebody else to realise theirs.

And it all started because of an interest in genealogy.

Fourteen years ago, Chris and I discovered a jailbird in the family tree and that moment in time triggered a series of events which changed our lives forever. It sent Chris and I on a quest which brought us even closer together and probably defined the second half of our marriage.

On top of this, thanks to Jamie Charlton, I have finally realised my ambition to become a published author and am now in a strong position to provide for myself and my children by doing a 'job' that I adore.

It is unlikely that I will ever pick up the genealogy trail again of the fractious Charlton family. It just wouldn't be the same without Chris. But I'm not too sad. I look back with love on the time Chris and I shared exploring his family's past; I'm proud of the stories we unearthed together. We were always a good team but we were an outstanding genealogical amateur partnership. I say a quiet 'thank you' every day for the journey we shared.

Despite the remoteness of our little corner of northern England, somehow our ancestors have always been in the thick of history. From the horrors of World War One, to the industrial revolution and the rise of Britain's railway industry, the Charltons have played their part. Even Jamie Charlton had a role in exposing the injustice of the early nineteenth century legal system. We may be descended from a bunch of 'churlish' thugs (who terrorized the Border region) and a notorious Regency criminal, but there is virtue and evil in every family, and over the generations the rough and the smooth have evened out.

Chris and I began this journey two decades ago with a light-hearted trip to a Northumbrian prison and ended up with a complex tale of real people which involved far more prisons and gaols than we ever imagined.

We wanted to create a unique history for ourselves and our children, and I think we've more than achieved this. We have explored the lives of three centuries of our ancestors and have uncovered salacious gossip, tragedy, kindness, loyalty, foolishness and bravery on a scale we could never imagine. It is not the (non-existent) money, wealth and status of our ancestors which moves us when we look back at the motley crew who passed down our surname and contributed the genetic makeup of our children; it is their fragile lives and fallible humanity which leaves such a lasting impression.

Understandably, at the moment, my children Beth and Ross still prefer to focus on the legacy of courage, love and support left to them by their incredible father. Everything they do in life is about pleasing his spirit and honouring his memory.

"I don't want to let Dad down," is a common refrain in our house.

But I have no doubt that when they're older, they will one day turn to the other legacy he left them: the story of the fascinating humanity of their ancestors.

One day my children will understand why this is so special.

Thank you for reading our story.
Karen Charlton
June 11th, 2018

AUTHOR NOTE

I wrote the first edition of *Seeking Our Eagle* in the spring of 2012, shortly after Chris's terminal diagnosis. Every now and then I went into the study and quietly spend a few hours on this project, looking back at our genealogical quest and the adventures we shared together.

I knew there was a lot of public interest in 'how we did it' and that's initially why I started this book, but as Chris battled for his life, *Seeking Our Eagle* became more than a just detailed account of a genealogical quest. It grew into my labour of love. It became a tribute to the most incredible man I've ever known. It's his biography and obituary rolled into one and my way of saying: 'I'll always love you.' It focuses on some of the happiest days of our marriage. I found comfort reminiscing about the laughs we'd enjoyed and the crazy things we did in pursuit of Jamie Charlton and his other ancestors. Writing *Seeking Our Eagle* was both escapism and a cathartic experience that helped me to cope with my grief.

Seeking Our Eagle was also the first book I self-published and the manuscript contained a lot of rookie mistakes in the formatting and style. It's taken me several years to find the time to correct this, hence this new edition. I also decided to take this opportunity to add *The Final Chapter* to the narrative to explain what happened to Chris, and why, sadly, there won't be a sequel to *Catching the Eagle.*

I know a lot of readers loved *Catching the Eagle* and will be disappointed but I hope that you understand why I can't dwell on the past any more, and must move forward. It hurts too much. The cosy, humorous, fictional world of Detective Stephen Lavender and Constable Ned Woods is where I'm happiest now – and where I find peace.

I hope you enjoyed our story and if you did, please leave *Seeking Our Eagle* a review on Amazon.

Karen Charlton,
Marske-by-the-Sea
North Yorkshire
June 11th, 2018

TOP TIPS FOR GENEALOGICAL RESEARCH

1. Make contact with all your living relatives and glean every bit of information you can from them.

2. ASSUME NOTHING. Absolutely nothing.

3. Don't be tight. Buy every birth, marriage and death certificate you can – it is amazing what you will miss otherwise.

4. Join genealogy websites, post your problems online and make use of the all the help available on their forums. Make online friends. Chat to people.

5. Be patient: the information you seek will eventually turn up. Failing that, join up with other interested family members and employ the services of a private researcher.

BIBLIOGRAPHY

Sand in my Shoes by James Mervyn Charlton

More Sand in my Shoes by James Mervyn Charlton

The Railways of Weardale by T. E. Routhwaite (1965)

The Monthly Chronicle of North-Country Law and Legend (1890), kindly sent to me by the Ponteland Local History Society

The court case notes 'The King v. Charlton' from The National Archives.

The Newcastle Courant: July 1809 – June 1811. Original Documents, Gateshead Central Library

Liberty is Sweet: wearsideonline.com

Printed in Great Britain
by Amazon

15334436R00079